Toltec Tools and Wisdom
How to Potty Train Your Brain

D1512068

Toltec Tools and Wisdom

How to
Potty Train
Your Brain

Diana D. Adkins

Editorial: Luis Cerda, Leslee Morrison

The Thinker image by Yair Haklai, published in Wikimedia Commons, was used and modified under the terms of the GNU Free Documentation License, Version 1.2 or any later version published by the Free Software Foundation wherein 'Permission is granted to copy, distribute and/or modify.

Also Available on Kindle!

ISBN-13: 978-1484867693

ISBN-10: 1484867696

To all those that seek,
know that you can find!

Table of Contents

Acknowledgments

Where I could, I have given credit to those I believe developed an idea, formula or definition. Yet, I don't always know that since students and teachers borrow, adapt and refine ideas as they grow; sharing and teaching others as they do.

I deeply honor the Toltec masters that taught, guided and supported me in the Toltec philosophy I share with you:

Don Juan Matus (as written of by Carlos Castaneda) was my first glimpse into the Toltec world.

Don Miguel Ruiz was my first direct experience of a Toltec Master. Don Miguel is an author, speaker, visionary and teacher in the Eagle Knight Lineage of Toltecs.

Gini Gentry - Worked closely with Don Miguel and is an author, speaker, visionary and teacher at her Garden of the Goddess center in New Mexico.

HeatherAsh Amara – Apprenticed with Don Miguel and Gini (among others) and was my first 'official' Toltec teacher, mentor, guide. She founded Toci-Toltec Center of Creative Intent where I received my certifications. She is an author, teacher and visionary who develops amazingly effective programs for self-awareness.

Raven Smith – Apprenticed with all of the above (among others) and he was my second official Toltec teacher, mentor and guide. Raven is also an author, teacher, visionary and program developer.

I have added my personal teachings in amongst the rest, but one thing about Toltecs is that we truly do our best to walk a path of Spirit, of the Warrior dedicated to awareness, personal mastery and integrity - sharing the knowledge and wisdom contained within Toltec philosophy to aid others in the awakening of consciousness.

Go Toltecs!

To my friends, editors, those that read this book for comments and those that suffered through my turmoil with cover design – your support and encouragement kept me going. Deb and Gary Marsh – you mean the world to me and your support, encouragement, critiques and inspiration mean more to me than I can ever say in words. Luis Cerda, Jim Morris and Leslee Morrison – you are amazing friends that have given me so much of your heart and support and I am so grateful. Anthony Flores, Bamma Kline, Skipper Derr, Arianna Fucini, Gracie Marsh, Tiffany Jama, Fatima Rigsby, Eric Derr, Paolo Caserta, Arielle Web, Susan Taylor, Lisa Bill, Maxine Missios, Suzanne

McBride, Chris Damon, Jeff Montondon, Julie Liegel, Renee Oglesbee, West Short and Judy York – thank you for your advice!

I'd also like to thank my SpiritWeavers students who have laughed and cried their way through these tools over the years, and who inspired me to give this book its name. You rock! Your courage and determination as you've potty trained your brains makes my heart sing! Thank you!

An Apology – Of Sorts

While researching potty training techniques, I noticed that potty training manuals assiduously avoided any specific reference to what potty training was designed to prevent. With children, as with our dogs, cats and other pets, it is clear that potty training is intended to do two things:

- Relieve parents and caregivers of the work and burden of keeping their charges clean and healthy, by

- Having the feces and urine going where it is less messy, more sanitary and out of sight - which for most of us is down the toilet.

As a culture, we avoid talking about feces and urine. The words themselves often make us feel unclean, yet their release from our bodies is a most natural and necessary function. This natural and necessary release is especially important in potty training our brains since, strangely, our brains tend to hold on to many things that should be flushed out and away.

So, here's the apology. We have to talk about excrement. If we are ever going to clean up the mess our brains make, we have to talk about the poo, poop, crap, and pee we hold on to. I could use the words feces and urine, but "cut the crap" is a phrase more readily understood than "cut the feces"!

To read and use the tools in this book, you will have to get over your aversion to looking at your own poop. Period. It is only through the awareness of what's really going on inside of us and our brains that we can create change. You can't change what you can't see. You have to stop turning away from all the crap you don't want to look at to finally clean it up; and flush it out and down the toilet - where it truly belongs.

Great! Now my apology is out of the way.....let's move on!

Part I – What's Going On (Truth, Lies and Parasites)

We've Got Issues

Most people in modern cultures are living lives dominated by their mind. We are constantly at the mercy of our mind's penchant for judging everything, making assumptions, comparing us with everyone else, projecting our hopes and fears onto other people and feeling victimized. Our minds are relentless, which is why so many traditions have taught meditation and quieting the mind for so many thousands of years – because we've got issues – mental issues.

Our minds aren't content with only what is conscious and easily seen, either. No, our minds bury piles of poo in our unconscious minds that also torment us. These arise as sudden feelings coming 'out of the blue', or unknown fears, anxiety and panic. So, we're often constipated - coming and going, inside and out. Given the piles of conscious *and* unconscious poo running through our brains, there is definitely a need to potty train it.

Another issue we have, that's again a mental manifestation, concerns our being somehow flawed. I could tell you that you were born a pure, incredibly amazing being; or that you were created in God's image and so you are truly magnificent, unique and divine – but you wouldn't believe me. You've been told this before, in many ways and traditions, and yet you'd still tell me that's a load of crap because you know, deep down, that you're not amazing or worthy - of love or hugs or wealth or success or attention or your dreams, or, or, or. Really, it's an endless stream of poo our minds throw at us every day of our lives; busily reminding us of every single insecurity and defect we've acquired in this lifetime. Some people would argue for past lifetimes as well!

Truly, if every sacred tradition or figure (including Jesus and Buddha) can't convince you, do I really stand a chance?

I had to ask myself that very question before writing this book. Do I stand any chance of convincing you that you really are unique and amazing - and that you are absolutely perfect (if just a little misguided in your penchant for beating yourself and everyone else up)?

I obviously decided I do since you're reading this. The truth is – there is no magic pill - yet there is a way out of the poo, because it truly is poo. My teachers have done it. I've done it. My colleagues have done it. My students have done it. And we're all regular people - just like you. So, if we can do it, I know you can, too.

And yes, it's OK if you don't believe me yet. Keep reading.

Potty train....*what?* Some of the facts involved.

Is there a difference between our mind and our brain? Many think they are the same thing, that our mind (how and what we think about things) is an activity of the brain and, therefore, the same. Others think of our brains as simply a large computer in our head that computes information, but that it isn't the same as our intellect and thoughts. There seems to be some truth to both ideas. I pulled out my "Webster's New World Dictionary" to check it out (copyright 1990 – yeah, it's old) and found:

- brain *n.* 1. the mass of nerve tissue in the cranium of the vertebrates. 2. [*often pl.*] intelligence.

- mind *n.* 1. memory. 2. opinion. 3. the seat of consciousness, in which thinking, feeling, etc. takes place. 4. intellect. 5. Psyche (*n. 2*). 6. reason, sanity.

At this point, let's just take a mental leap and accept that the concepts of intelligence, intellect and reason are so similar as to be interchangeable insofar as this book goes, shall we? I'll say brain or mind and you'll get the picture.

Furthermore, my research on brain development also supports the thesis that there is less separation between mind and brain than one might think. If you study the subject, be prepared to learn about the stages of neural development, neurotransmitters, synapses and a whole lot more that can sometimes be, well...*boring*!

I found interesting information, however, that is helpful to understand here and that speaks to the interrelatedness between mind and brain that will relate to potty training *your* brain:

- Many new parents talk to and play music for their 'not yet born child' because studies have shown that the fetus (and its brain) is affected by all of the environmental conditions it experiences - not simply nutrition.

- From the moment we are born, the brain is a work in progress. Our brains will change over time as we learn, grow and experience life.

- Our experiences in life, from birth onward, begin to take over from our genetic make-up by adding, changing and modifying our original genetic predispositions. Our life experiences trigger and stimulate our brain's development as we grow.

- The route from short term to long term memory is repetition. Regularly repeated experiences and thoughts cause neural pathways and connections to become *permanently etched in our brains.*

- Practice makes perfect....or *permanent*...in the case of brain and neural development.

- Starting around 10 years of age and continuing through our teens, our brains begin to discard neural connections that are not used. Strong or frequently used connections aren't weeded out.

- While our brain becomes stronger, more focused and more powerful as we grow older (having fewer connections to channel through), we also become more 'stuck' and are less able to adapt to our changing environment.

- Once our brain's neural networks and pathways stabilize, we have developed our own personal patterns of behavior and thought, action and reaction.

- "A baby born with a potential for greatness encoded in his genes may turn out to have a gift for logic or a brilliant criminal mind, the direction defined by his early experiences. – Nash, J.M.

(1997). How a child's brain develops. Time Magazine, 3 February.

Whew! This information is enough to scare any parent witless! The fact that our *brains* develop as they do, dependent upon our early life experiences, is an awesome responsibility for those in charge of those early experiences.

We did, however, know that...didn't we? Many have blamed their lives on our parents, but blaming our **brains** on them? And, let's face it, we have all blamed our parents for some aspect of our lives. If only Dad had been home more. If only my parents had been more loving. If my Mother had breast fed me longer, I wouldn't be insecure. If I was more secure I wouldn't need those implants...or Viagra...or be afraid of women...or afraid of men...or of relationships, or...or...or...*oy!*

The information about brain development is not a free pass to blame our parents for how we've turned out. Period! It's simply giving us some ideas of the work ahead of us, especially since, by eighteen years old, we are less able to adapt.

Potty Training Basics

One of the first rules of potty training is to wait until you and the child (read 'brain' here) are ready. Familydoctor.org says that, "You are ready when you are able to devote the time and energy necessary to encourage your child on a daily basis." That's true for kids and brains. So, let's assume that, since you're reading this book, you might be ready. Or if not, then you will be by the time we're done!

Your brain, on the other hand, will never be ready. It likes its beliefs, rules, programs and definitions. It likes its control. It wants to be safe and right, which means maintaining the status quo that can drive us so very crazy. Ugh! More on this in the next chapters – just keep the faith!

Doing research into potty training humans was quite interesting, especially since my only experience involved pets and my own brain. I found it amusing to see how the principals for potty training children, pets and brains overlapped. I discovered a site that gave ten steps to prepare for potty training.

1. Have bathroom breaks together. (We take our brains everywhere with us, so this is a no-brainer.)

2. Support your child to understand the difference between ready to 'go', going and, oops – I just went! (This is about awareness, awareness, awareness and gets into some interesting concepts covered later.)

3. Let your child go nude when they can so they can see what's happening. (OK…this could be *FUN!*)

4. Make time to potty train. (Yes, yes, yes!)

5. Find the right throne. (*Huh?*)

6. Heap on praise and rewards. (Absolutely essential in potty training your brain.)

7. Turn it into target practice. (OK…we'll define 'targets' differently here, but you've got to love this one!)

8. Support your child's creativity and imagination. (Definitely an essential for the brain, too.)

9. Prepare for adventures. (Yay! Let's play!)

10. Go for it! (Why not? You are going to live life anyway, so why not go for it?)

Potty training your brain can be as simple or as complex as you make it. Cleaning up your poo can be a painful chore or an amusing adventure, all depending upon you. The truth is that it is often both. Once you begin to clean up some of the poo, however, you're able to see the benefits and can actually laugh when life 'brings it on'! Here comes another movement! Yay! Flush that poop!

Who Created this Mess and What's a Toltec?

If you read the back cover or acknowledgments for this book, you know that I am a Toltec teacher, minister, coach and Toltec team player. The Toltecs, however, didn't create the mess humanity's brains finds themselves in. Fortunately for us, the Toltec's study of human development figured a way out of the proverbial 'shit'. They made this discovery by keenly observing human nature, on both a physical level and an energetic one. Early Toltecs didn't ask 'why' humans create so much poo as much as they looked at how and what we did to create it, and the effects it had on ourselves and others.

Here is a general run-down of relevant Toltec concepts:

Domestication

Much like our pets and animals, humans are 'domesticated'. We usually get uncomfortable with this phrase because we consider ourselves above it all, but the truth is – we're domesticated.

My handy Webster's defines 'domesticate' as: *vt*. 1. to accustom to home life. 2. to tame for human use.

Yes, we have most certainly been domesticated and tamed for home and human use!

As revealed earlier, even before birth, our parents and environment have an influence on us. Once we're born, the domestication begins in earnest. We learn everything our family has to teach us. We are dry sponges, soaking up everything around us. We're told how to 'be' to be acceptable within our family, religion, culture and society. We're trained as to what's right and wrong and what's appropriate to think, say, fear, believe, eat, wear, study, do, not do and so on.

All of this training is designed to keep us safe and behaving correctly – as our parents, religion, culture and society deem these concepts to be – not necessarily how *we* deem these to be. Yet as young children, we lap it up because our parents are on par with God at that age and of course they know what's best for us….right?

Usually, our domestication is accomplished through a system of punishment and reward. If you were 'good', you'd get smiles, hugs, love and approval from your parents. If you were 'bad' you'd get frowns, disapproval and their withholding of hugs and love (or a 'time out' if you were lucky). Many that didn't get 'time outs' received a spanking, switching, yelling, beating or worse....all of them.

To a young child, the withholding of love and approval can literally feel like death, just like a beating can. Young children are completely dependent upon their caregivers for food, shelter, love and safety. If any of these essentials are withheld, complete panic can set in, along with an overwhelming desire to feel safe and loved – which usually results in the child's compliance. This is why 'punishment and reward' is such an effective training tool.

Notice, though, that I said 'feel' safe and loved. Children develop many ideas around what safety means, and their *feeling* safe does not always equate with *being* safe. Sometimes it is 'safe enough' to simply hide so you're not punished while the parent, teacher or sibling continues to do their thing. Hiding may still not be safe.

This is where the 'games' began. This is where the shit started. Despite the usually well-meaning efforts of our parents, 'punishment and reward' taught us to crave that which makes us happy, unafraid and safe – and to avoid or deny that which makes us unhappy, fearful or unsafe.

Book of Law – or 'The Rules'

As young children grow through domestication, they are taught the rules of life. They also make up their own rules through personal experiences. All of these rules get written into our internal 'Book of Law' or 'Book of Life' that we carry with us – always. *Everything* gets recorded in this book, which is where the computer aspect of our brain excels. Whether we consciously remember an incident or not, the rules we create from our experiences are written in our book, and they are incredibly efficient at controlling our reality.

Remember, repeated experiences cause pathways to become permanently etched in our brains. Repetition is the key that moves short-term memory into long-term memory. It's similar to remembering a new phone number. At first, you have to write it down to remember it. Once you've repeated it a few times, it becomes 'etched' in your brain. It doesn't take more than a few 'whacks' for us to learn what to do - *or a few hugs*.

Here's a story I learned from HeatherAsh that we call the 'Vase Story', which illustrates how easily, and deceptively, rules get written in our books:

Let's imagine ourselves to be young children, and in this case we're all little girls with a little brother (sorry

guys, you can reverse the roles and still get the message.).
Let's also imagine that we've had an amazing, loving
mother that's never punished us. OK, got the fantasy?

One day your Mom was having a really, really bad day.
She was yelled at by her boss for something she didn't do;
her car wouldn't start and when it did it meant she hit
rush hour traffic about the time her air conditioner broke
and the chocolate she'd bought melted on the car seat.
Then, the babysitter called to tell her that since Mom was
now thirty minutes late, she absolutely *had* to leave to
catch her plane and the kids would only be alone for five
minutes. Now, on top of everything, Mom was also scared
for her kids.

The babysitter leaves with an admonition to the
children to not open the door for anyone (no matter what),
and to stay out of the kitchen – period. The kids,
experiencing a moment of unparalleled freedom, agree
and begin to play tag around the house as the babysitter
locks the door and leaves.

Brother and sister are having a grand time playing tag.
As brother zips around the hallway, sister on his heels, his
hand accidentally knocks over a vase on the table. It falls
off and breaks on the floor, and his little sister jumps over
it and continues to chase him because - this is fun!

A couple of minutes later, Mom frantically comes home after her truly horrendous day and opens the door to find the vase her Mother gave her, right before she died, lying broken in pieces on the hallway floor. Do you think Mom stayed calm? No way! The kids come careening around the corner and stop dead in their tracks.

The wonderful, loving Mom they knew is spitting mad and looks as if some demon has taken possession of her. For the first time ever, Mom *yells*, "Who broke my vase?" In shock, brother points to sister and says, "She did!" You start to protest, but Mom doesn't want to hear it. She points at you and says, "Go to your room! NOW!" Crying, you flee the monster that was once your Mother and go to your room. Brother has a smirk on his face, but Mom tells him, "You – go watch TV."

So, in tears and scared to death, you go to your room. Is it likely you'll think that Mom must have had a bad day and she just temporarily lost it? No, not likely at your age. What you do is cry. You feel how unfair Mom is being. You didn't break the vase, brother did, but you're the one being punished and yelled at. You feel very, very confused, hurt, scared and sorry for yourself. Your brain agonizes over it all, *and it begins to make up stories to explain what happened.*

This example illustrates how our personal beliefs start to be written. First, you could have the idea that Mom loves brother more, since she obviously listened to him and not you. Then you might consider that boys are liars. It becomes obvious that playing and having fun is a bad, bad, *BAD* thing. Equally obvious is that girls are not as good as boys because Mom didn't believe you. Are you getting the picture here?

Now, begin to imagine the *rules* that could be written from the beliefs created by this one incidence; and guys, just reverse boys for girls:

Belief	Rule/Law
boys get more love than girls	I have to work extra hard for love
boys are more important than girls	give in to boys, let them win
boys are liars	never believe a word boys say
boys get preferential treatment	I'm a girl so I deserve to be treated badly
playing causes problems	never, *ever*, have too much fun
girls shouldn't run	track is out

I am a bad person   I'll just give up now

I don't deserve Mom's   no one will ever love me
love

The list can go on and on, all of it developing beliefs, rules and agreements that get recorded in the 'Book of Law' that we carry through life with us.

Selective Evidence Gathering

Mom cools down and fixes dinner for everyone and comes to get you from your room. She apologizes for yelling at you and says she's sorry. You, however, have now developed beliefs and agreements about the way things are, and you don't believe her. You now *know* that she loves brother more. As a result, at dinner, you will see her passing the potatoes to brother first as evidence to support this belief. Because you now *know* she loves brother more, you will not even notice that she later passes the spinach to you first.

Our brains will filter out any and all evidence that does not support the beliefs and agreements we have made.

This is selective evidence gathering. As this child (you) goes through life, imagine what sort of relationships you'll have, especially with boys, if you believe that men are liars and they'll betray you, or that you don't deserve love? *Now* are you getting the picture?

Cognitive Dissonance

What happens, as we go through life and our Book of Law gets written, is that we develop contradicting laws, beliefs and rules. At six you might have been told repeatedly that children were meant to be seen and not heard, and this rule (or 'law') gets written on page seventy of your Book of Law. After a few years, you've got the message ingrained in your brain and the resulting rule (don't speak up) is so normal that it fades into your subconscious and you become a quiet child. You then enter your teens and things change. Now your teachers, friends and dates start telling you to speak up for yourself, to be seen *and* heard. Yikes! While not speaking up helped you to navigate your home life, the rule would not serve you if you wanted to excel at school, join the debate team or have dates and lots of friends.

Another example from American culture is one from way back in the '60's. At that time, most people were raised to believe that sex before marriage was bad, wrong, a sin and they'd go to hell if they tried it. That got written on, say, page one hundred of their Book of Law. They lived happily along until the '70's arrived with its 'free love, sex and rock 'n' roll' and 'love the one you're with'.

These agreements now get written on page two hundred in their Book of Law – that it's OK and 'groovy' to love the one you're with.

These two very different sets of rules create problems when they begin to fight it out between themselves. If folks followed the latter and loved the one they were with, the former agreement that they were going to hell for doing so would rise up and war would ensue. They would be doing what their new belief said was fine, while their old belief was screaming hell-fire and brimstone at them. Guilt and shame would result. Their internal judge/critic would have a field day and they'd end up a miserable wreck, totally confused at how something so groovy could feel so bad.

This 'fight' between our old rules and our new rules creates a mental (cognitive) disagreement (dissonance). We believe two or more conflicting rules and they are all trying to determine our behavior. It's confusing, and this confusion can arise from very deep levels within us because we don't always remember the old rules. They were buried in our subconscious years ago, yet are still operating today. Confusion, insecurity, shame and guilt often arise as a result of the cognitive dissonance we feel when competing or contradictory rules from our Book of

Law start to argue. I bet you can come up with a few of your own about now.

Another example: we're all taught that fire burns. That's recorded around page twenty in everyone's Book of Law. In comes Fire Walking; an ancient practice in many cultures but relatively new to people living in the States. Well, I'm sure you can imagine the mind is now going, "Are you crazy? You really *do* have shit for brains if you think you can walk across fire and not get burned!" People are taught how to fire walk safely, yet still go into fear before the walks as a result of the conflicting rules and information – fire burns _and_ yes, you can walk on fire. (In this case, both are true under different circumstances. Many people have fire-walked and still have 'happy feet' - like mine!)

The point of this chapter is that each of us has conflicting rules and beliefs written throughout our Book of Law. Until these agreements reach the light of day, they're arguing and fighting it out in the battlefield of our brains and bodies, causing us to feel guilt, anger, confusion and shame – *often without knowing why*. Without truly looking at our lives and the beliefs and agreements we've accepted or created, we remain clueless about many of the feelings that arise within us. Cognitive dissonance is one hint that there's something to examine here. Keep this in mind as you read on.

A Look at our Brains and Strategies to Survive

Being the domesticated, creative beings that we are, we devise strategies to cope with our beliefs and agreements. Young children are quite amazing and especially creative, and before they prune away neural connections in their teens, they possess more 'brain matter' than their parents. From the research I shared earlier, remember:

- From *the moment we are born*, the brain is a work in progress.

- Our life experiences (especially those in early childhood) trigger our brain's development as we grow.

- Practice (repetition) makes perfect....or *permanent...* in the case of brain and neural development.

- Starting around 10 years of age (and continuing through our teens), our brains begin to reject and throw out neural connections *that are not used*. Strong or frequently used connections aren't affected – which means that we keep them.

- Once our brain's neural networks stabilize, we have developed our personal patterns of behavior, thought, action and reaction.

Information like the above is what makes me believe child rearing to be the most important job on the planet!

Given the extraordinarily creative nature of children and the influence of domestication, is it any wonder that they develop strategies to handle the world they find themselves in, and one they eventually co-create for themselves?

Any parent can tell you what some of the strategies are. Heck, most of us could tell you, too, since we develop strategies as children, and yet maintain them as adults. A baby cries to get the breast (As do some adults, yes?). Kids smile sweetly to gain approval (Practice makes permanent, right?). Some kids throw tantrums to gain attention (As do some adults, so I rest my case!).

There is another way of looking at the strategies we develop. It is intended to give you a general understanding of strategies and to help you ascertain what strategies you took on. You have probably developed one primary strategy, with others that compliment and support the primary. Here's the general idea:

- Controller – this strategy takes charge of the people and the world around it to get approval and stay safe. Do it my way and all will be OK, right?

- Pleaser – pleasing involves taking care of other people, helping everyone, and making everyone around you happy so that you are rewarded, loved and not punished. Here, let me take care of your every need and you'll love me, right?

- Distracter – this strategy keeps attention directed away from you to stay safe by redirecting it anywhere and everywhere else. Moving targets are harder to hit, yes?

- Isolator – an isolator hides, hides, hides and figures 'out of sight, out of mind' is a great way to stay safe. You can't hit what you can't see!

With these survival mechanisms also come sub-categories. For example, I was a rebel. Underneath my pleasing/controlling, I was rebelling. I'd make you happy so you wouldn't notice I was sneaking out the backdoor to meet my boyfriend. Others are conformers and will go along with everything so they blend in – whether they agree or not. It's easier and safer to just say yes, than it is to actually rebel…yes?

For kids, these strategies work really well. We gain approval and are relatively safe from the disapproval of our parents, caregivers and society at large. Once practiced repeatedly, however, our strategies become permanent – operating far beyond childhood and into adulthood, where not all of us appreciate being controlled, care-taken, distracted, ignored or rebelled against!

The Parasite

'Parasite' is a disturbing word, and Toltecs use it to describe an understandable (yet disturbing) relationship we all participate in within ourselves – usually unconsciously. I say 'understandable' because once you've gotten all the basics, it makes unfortunate 'sense' that we are the way we are – as crappy as that sometimes feels.

Webster wasn't helpful here, as it simply says a parasite is one who lives at others' expense without making any useful return. While the Parasite does live at our expense, our Parasites *were* useful...once.

Toltecs define our Parasite as a combination of our Book of Law, our Judge and our Victim – and we all have a Parasite within us. The Parasite's primary goal is to keep us safe and to keep itself right – period – but usually as our five (or three or ten) year old self defined the words 'safe' and 'right'.

You would do well to remember that last line, since its importance cannot be stressed enough. *Your Parasite's primary goal is to keep you safe and right – no matter what.* This strategy was critical for us as children, but as we grow older, it starts to hinder us, usually at the expense of the life we lead: the people, love, amount of money, success, failure, job and friends that we do, and don't, have.

You now understand the Book of Law concept, and probably have some ideas about your own Book of Law. You've heard the Vase Story, and have seen how beliefs, rules and agreements get made. The remaining two components of the Parasite - the Judge and Victim - should be a breeze for you!

The Judge gets its start from the external judges in our life. As children we're told what's good and what's bad. We learn the 'good' judgments and are rewarded for being good little boys and girls. We're also told when we're 'bad' boys and girls and we are then punished accordingly. If we do what we're told, we're good. If we rebel, disobey or get too creative – we're bad. It's really this simple. This domestication, combined with our creative ability to make up and internalize stories about our experiences, result in our Judge.

As we go through life, the external judges in our lives become internalized voices in our heads. We've learned our lessons well, and through repetition we've etched them firmly in our brains. We no longer need our parents, teachers or peers to tell us when we're being good or bad. We do it all on our own, over and over again, and often ad nauseam. Remember, repeated experiences create well worn pathways, permanently etched into our brain, so the lessons, criticism, judgments, comparisons and beliefs soon become internal tyrants that never let up or give us a break.

At The Child Development Institute I learned that: "Children are not little adults. Until they reach the age of 15 or so, they are not capable of reasoning as an adult." What?! How interesting (and scary) is that! Piaget's classic *Stages of Cognitive Development*, also tells us that in the Intuitive Phase (roughly 4-7 years old), kids tend to focus their attention on only one aspect of any object/thing while ignoring others. The thoughts and ideas they form are crude (they're only six!), they are often irreversible (darn!) and it's easy for them to believe in magic since reality (at that age) is not yet firmly established. Piaget says that in this stage, a child's perceptions dominate their judgment, which means that what they perceive (feel, understand and then think) creates their judgments. A child feeling badly about something could turn into the *child perceiving itself* as 'bad' – just as being told to be 'seen and not heard' could result in the child believing that to speak up at all is 'bad'. Piaget goes on to state that for this stage, children use the 'do's and don'ts' imposed by parents, society and authority figures *to determine their self-perception*. Yikes!

For children (until our early to mid teens apparently), there isn't enough cognitive development yet to separate our *actions* as being bad from *ourselves* as being bad. How we perceive things, how they feel or 'look', dominates our judgment. Our parents/teachers/society/peers tell us we're good or bad, and we believe it. We hear it often enough, and the litany creates a tape *that plays and repeats on its own in our heads* – I'm bad, broken, unworthy, un-loveable, not good enough/strong enough/cool enough, I'm too much, too weak, too little, too weird – and we no longer need the external judges. We've created an internal judge that is usually far meaner and stricter than those outside of us. A person can pass away but their voice in our head keeps judging us on and on. We are judged coming and going, inside and out. Eventually, we believe we must, somehow, be guilty as charged.

From the Judge, the Victim is created. Our victim is a response to the judge, and its role involves avoiding responsibility and blaming anything (or anyone) else for what's going on.   Our Parasites want to stay safe, remember, so it's easier if everything is someone (or something) else's fault. *Life seems so much easier that way.*

The voice of the victim sounds like: but it's not fair; it's not my fault; you made me mad/cry/hurt; the devil made me do it; my childhood is to blame; I can't help it; if only I was richer, smarter, more handsome, beautiful, in shape, skinny, strong, funny, serious, cooler, weirder - then things would be OK, or this wouldn't be happening.   Get the picture? If not, think of someone in your life – and we all have them – who is continually complaining about how they aren't to blame for what's going on and that it's always someone else's fault.   The victim doesn't take responsibility.

I've focused on the 'bad' judgments more than the 'good' because they are well known and get the point across. They're all still judgments, though - the good and the bad. 'Good' judgments also create problems. If you believe it is 'good' to be perfectly groomed, you'll often discount those that aren't and avoid them.   Imagine Einstein with his wild hair! You'd pass him by, dismissing him as ill groomed because you would be too 'good' to even talk to him.

One of mine is honesty. I believe it is right and in my integrity to be honest. It would get twisted, however, if I then turned around and judged everyone I *thought* was being dishonest. I could be selectively gathering my evidence, maybe my caretaker got engaged, or more likely, my controller. I'd have to fix them or show them the error of their ways. This response is one of the traps that groups, cultures and nations often fall into.

Believing your beliefs and ideas are 'good' is one thing. Problems arise, however, when we insist that everyone else must believe them, too, and do it our way - or else.

Self-Importance

Everyone has to deal with self-importance, so let go of any ideas that I might not mean you.

Self-importance arises when you believe that a situation (person, the world) revolves around you and your opinions, and that you are right. There are the obvious examples of arrogance and self-importance that we can all see, the 'I'm better than' type, but there are others that are equally destructive.

Self-importance can mean thinking that you (or an idea/belief) are the best, smartest or strongest. That's the easy one to see. It can also be about being the worst, lowest, and weakest. That's right, being the worst, having the worst day, the worst life, the worst illness, the weakest body, the most dreadful experience – are all examples of self-importance. Some people are trying to win an award for being the best – even if winning means being the best at the worst!

Every time we try to control, fix, change someone's mind and take care of other people/things, we have fallen into self-importance to some degree. We think we know what's right and best. We often do it in the name of love, in the guise of compassion, duty or honor. We rationalize our behavior, saying that it's in someone's best interest; that they aren't smart enough or don't know what they really want and so of course someone has to look out for them – often without asking them or gaining their permission.

This behavior, essentially, invalidates the other person and their thoughts, ideas and opinions. It puts us above them, makes us 'better or smarter or more able than' they are and it is the height of self-importance. What we're doing is really very selfish and arrogant. We are trying to make them into our own image or idea of what's right, rather than allowing them to grow and develop their own ideas and image.

Many of the caretakers trying to make the world a better place are probably yelling at me right now, along with a lot of parents, officials, presidents and controllers. That's OK. Yell. I'm not saying that parents shouldn't instill beliefs in their children. It's OK; you can't avoid domesticating them. Work ethics and codes of conduct are essential in businesses, too. However, we are caught in self-importance if we believe that we are right, they are wrong, and that we know what other people want and need. Period. Our 'right' is right for *us*, but not necessarily everyone else. Think about how you feel when someone insists that you change and do things their way. It's not pretty or fun! In fact, you'd probably like to throttle them, yes?

Have you ever considered the acronym for 'we are right'? *It is W.A.R.* Think about it. Please.

Remember choice? Everyone has a right to make their own choices, mistakes and successes. Byron Katie states it well when she says that there is God's business, other's business and your business – and the only place you should stick your nose is in yours! Having said that, if someone *asks* you for help or for your opinion – great! Tell them, help them, counsel them and educate them as to your views, knowledge, experience and expertise – because *they asked.*

There are also many ways we choose to work with someone else's ideas of 'right and wrong', and that's fine.

For example, when we sign up for classes, college and retreats we are asking to be taught and it is implied that we will follow the rules. When we choose to work for someone, we're agreeing to follow the company's rules and ideas of what's right for that company. Parents with adult kids living at home often have 'house rules' for living there. All of these are fine since we are making conscious decisions for what we're choosing to do with ourselves. Self-importance, however, arises when we believe our ideas are right for everyone, and then we judge or try to make everyone else conform to what we believe is right.

Disaster Mind

Disaster mind is a rather strange aspect of our brain and parasite. As far as I can tell, it is truly crazy - at least mine is. Maybe it's too many movies and TV shows, but my mind can envision a disaster in an instant. I'll be driving home, and suddenly my mind is imagining that 18-wheeler having simultaneous blow-outs and careening into my lane to hit me head on. Yikes!

The guys go off on a hunting trip, and their partners envision them dead in the woods. The women go off for a girl's night out, and their partners see them in bed with someone else. Your kids are late coming home from school, and now the bus has had an accident or some stalker grabbed them. Or, you'll imagine an argument with someone. Or, you'll think a friend sees you in a store, but they keep walking so you imagine they're mad at you. Or, you'll hear a noise in the night and be positive someone is breaking into your house, even though the squirrels have simply returned to the tree by your window.

Are you getting the idea? Disaster mind isn't an accident waiting to happen – it's a full blown, often over the top, created scenario that has no basis in reality! So there!

Yet, people actually believe this poop! "I know that Jane is mad at me because she was short on the phone." Excuse me? What if Jane was distracted or her boss just walked up? "My Mom just gave me 'the look' so I know I'm in trouble." Hold up here! What if she was simply puzzling over what birthday gift to give you? It's possible! Some of you will argue with me that I'm wrong and that you *know.* OK…give it your best shot, but I'll let the words of Mark Twain say it all:

"I am an old man and have known a great many troubles, ***but most of them never happened."***

We do this *all the time.* Our minds create stories, scenes and outcomes from our fears, judge and victim that haven't happened, never happen, and usually aren't remotely true! And yet, we suffer them. We agonize over them. We fear them. Dear God/dess, what if our fears really happened? Then our disaster mind picks up *that* story line, too – that the disaster really has happened - and suddenly we're doubly disaster screwed! The partner really is in bed with a stranger, they're going to fall in love, I'll be left devastated and I'll never find another partner as good as that one so I'll be alone and life won't be worth living...and on and on and on. This, surely, is a definition of insanity.

Lies

The most definitive moment that drew me to the Toltec path was the instant Don Miguel Ruiz told a group of us in Santa Fe that most of what was going on in our heads was a lie. That's right, a *lie*. The proverbial light bulb lit up in my brain as his words resonated deeply within me. I knew I had just heard a truth.

While 'lies' is strongly put, and a bit of a tough word, it nevertheless points to a truth – that most of what we *believe* is a lie. Most of what we've been *told* in our lives is a lie, too. *Everyone* filters their perceptions through their domestication, Parasite and selective evidence gathering. So, while people might truly believe that what they are telling you is the truth – it doesn't mean that it is. The most we could say is that it is *their* truth. Period.

Yeah, I know. You're probably listing right now all the truths that you know to be true. Yet are they? With science surging where no wo/man has gone before, can you be sure of any alleged 'truth'? The table you think is solid, isn't, fire doesn't always burn, the world isn't flat. The beliefs you hold aren't necessarily even yours, so are they true for you?

Every single thing we believe to be true might not be. Yay! Maybe you're not bad - you are simply being human! *What a relief!* A new world of magic, wonder and curiosity can open up for you – as long as you don't hold onto the belief that you are right. If you will simply allow a wee possibility that you might just be wrong – everything can open up for you. Life can become an amazing path of discovery rather than a routine, mundane path of existence.

Yes, folks - most of what we believe is a lie. Our truth is what we choose it to be. If you choose to believe self-limiting poo - you will make it your truth because - as we think, we create. And while there appear to be real truths – this is still up to each of us to discover for ourselves. People do walk on fire, some Tibetans leap incredible heights, some people have ESP, Buddha became enlightened, Jesus walked on water and said we could, too - so don't let your domestication restrict your potential!

The Dream of the Planet

Many look at people and the world around us and think, "Wow, that's crazy! Who'd ever think that? What the hell do they think they're doing, anyway? That's just wrong!" While we, of course, are absolutely sane. It's a function of our Parasite to be right, right? So, of course it's going to tell us that we're sane in the midst of all the craziness.

So, let's take a closer look at what we call 'sanity'. Sanity is another concept that has been defined by our parents, culture and society. In western cultures, we often question our self-worth (and think that it's perfectly sane to do so); yet in Tibetan cultures they can't conceive of such a thing! To them, *that* is insane since they are taught that every life has tremendous value. Many cultures are taught the value of *every single life* – and that includes animals, plants, insects and earth. Yet those of us born and raised in a western, modern cultures are rarely taught the concept. We place humans at the head of the line, pets second, food animals next, and everything else so distant down the track as to be expendable.

My lovely Webster's says: sane *adj.* 1. mentally healthy; rational. 2. sound; sensible.

Who decides what rational, sound, sensible and mentally healthy actually mean? John C. Lilly, M.D., for one, coined a phrase that I find describes our *ideas* of 'sane' clearly: *Human Consensus Reality.* That's right, human consensus reality. This means that a group of humans agree on what's right and what's not and that becomes the bar for both reality and sanity.

If you don't buy into this reality, you're crazy, right? The problem is, reality changes given where you live and what you believe. Many Americans believe Californians and their economics are nuts. Aboriginal cultures *know* we are crazy. Some believe war is crazy, while others think it is essential. Most religions teach their adherents to think that other faiths (than theirs) are either wrong or way off the mark. Democrats think Republicans are nuts, and vice versa. This list could go on and on, but essentially, sanity is defined by what groups of people have chosen to believe that it is - **whether it is true or not**.

Where people disagree, well, that's when wars start – between countries, religions, ideas, friends, families – you get the picture. Everyone has their idea of reality and what is right. Remember W.A.R.?

Human consensus reality, with all of its vagaries and inconsistencies, is what Toltecs call the 'Dream of the Planet'. The Dream of the Planet in the United States (also known as 'The American Dream') has been that: you went to school, made good grades, got a good job, married a good person, had good kids, bought a good car and house, had credit card bills and a mortgage and worked hard all of your life to pay for it all until you retired and then you could relax and do everything you didn't have time to do while you worked so hard. Whew! People that didn't conform to the American Dream were considered odd-balls, eccentrics or radicals to be suspicious of, pitied or rejected.

Fear arises when we're suspicious, and fear usually walks hand-in-hand with disaster mind. With the stock market, banking and housing crashes, fear wildly escalated in the United States. World economics have been threatened and many dreams on the planet appear endangered. Globally, fear has now become another Dream of the Planet paradigm, and many are buying into it.

The Dream of the Planet changes from place to place and culture to culture, but it is still essentially a dream. Those living outside of the American Dream had their own visions for life. Some preferred to not 'keep up with the

Jones'. They didn't believe that they needed the things (house, car, clothes) to be acceptable. They didn't want their life choices dictated by bills and banks. Some joined communities, some moved to the wilds and still others found the middle path through all of the extremes. Not everyone buys into the Dream of Fear, either. Many have faith in their religious tradition and faith in their God, their government or themselves to weather whatever storms may arise. They relax in that faith so that fear doesn't find them an easy target.

Understand that humans constantly dream - awake and asleep, collectively and individually. We have our personal dreams, ideas and goals that we strive for. Some people believe in the collective dreams and promises that everything will be OK if we follow certain rules. Unfortunately, people often make shit up and then call it reality, call it sane - an example being the recent banking and real estate deceit in the U.S.A. Yet truly, what we call reality is a dream, changeable and variable, and we are each dreamers creating our dream. Keep reading, because this is a good thing! If you create your dream, then you can re-create and re-envision it for yourself!

How They All Play Together

All of these aspects of our strange but real brains find the sandbox called 'us' a delight.   We're so very responsive! We get emotional! We react! We believe our poo and then we actually *act* on it!

The very act of responding and acting keeps our Parasite alive and fully in control.   Practice makes permanent, remember? The rules are written. The Judge jumps on us at the slightest transgression.   The Victim exclaims in self-defense that it isn't our fault.   Disaster mind keeps the horrors alive for us. The dreams fall short, fear gets engaged and our strings get jerked, over and over again.

The very act of *thinking* all this poo-poo continues to etch the pathways even more indelibly in our brains and lives. You've got to get this one: *THE VERY ACT OF THINKING ALL THIS CRAP ETCHES THE PATHWAYS INDELIBLY IN OUR MINDS AND LIVES!*

By the time we're twenty, there's a wide boulevard for thoughts to travel down. Of course we've failed – didn't our parents, teachers, friends and mind tell us we would? Of course we're unworthy – we don't have the body, clothes, car, house, partner or job that we 'should'. People have died or abandoned us so we must be unlovable. We didn't follow our dreams so we're not strong, smart or courageous enough. Of course we won't succeed – doesn't our disaster mind create horrible scenarios if we even *think* of making changes – on top of our fears and lack of self-worth?

Richard Bach said it beautifully in his book, *Illusions*: "Argue for your limitations, and sure enough, they're yours." Think about this one because, as you'll see, you are choosing your reality.

Awareness and Choice ~ or ~ It's All Yours!

Whew! There's a lot of information above for you to assimilate! If I were you, I'd take a walk and feel into it. Maybe have a cup of tea. Relax, take a breather. I'm here to tell you that potty training your brain is not impossible to do and that there is hope. There is a way out of your poop.

The very first step is awareness. Remember – you can't change what you can't see. Awareness of the dream you're dreaming and the levels of poop you're carrying around is the first step. Awareness is *everything*, and one of the Toltec's first masteries. That's right, mastery.

To get there, you have to begin to look at what's actually running around your brain. Doing so requires a level of attention we don't usually apply to our thoughts and our poo. It also requires that we not avoid, deny, distract, please, control and deflect ourselves from our intent to actually look at ourselves. There are piles of poo in there, and once you find them, you can learn to clean them up and flush them out.

We have been domesticated, remember, to run away from anything that hurts or makes us uncomfortable because that's not safe. I'd say our shit qualifies here. Any pain or discomfort, to our Parasites, equals something to be protected from. Consequently, we have spent years of our lives not looking at half of it! We spend so much time avoiding the icky poo, that we have it down to a science of deflection. Let's see, I think I'll look at this argument I had to see if I can figure out why I thought or reacted the way I did….but wouldn't a nap be great first? How about a beer or a glass of wine, a piece of cake or a cigarette? Before you know it, the impetus to look at your poo pile has been deflected and you're off to the next idea, or the next TV show or phone call. You have been stopped dead in your tracks and your parasite has won…again.

Another trick our Parasite uses to keep itself safe and right is the Victim's voice. I personally loved to 'chew' on things. Like a dog, I'd get something (or someone) in my teeth and wouldn't let go because, of course, it was "all their fault"! As a strategy of deflection, it worked great to keep me focused on them, and not on myself. One of the greatest tools I used to re-focus myself was: when I found myself 'chewing' on someone or something and totally focused on them/it (rather than on myself/me), was to use the old saying – *if you point a finger at someone else, three are pointing back at you.* Try it. Hold your hand up and point your finger (and no, not your middle one, goofus!). There are three fingers pointing back at you and they are your clue as to where your attention needs to be - firmly on yourself and not on anyone else.

The simple truth is that: You are 100% responsible for your (own) reality. (Gulp!) This is a very hard pill for most folks to swallow. I'm responsible for my reality!? *All of it?*

Yes, you are. Resistance is futile, so if you give it up now, this will all go a lot easier and you'll be much happier in the long run. I promise!

We have been domesticated into blaming others. We were blamed, and we learned to blame. It is so much easier to blame anything and anyone else rather than assume responsibility for ourselves. It keeps the Parasite alive within us and keeps us right and safe if what's happening is someone else's fault and we aren't in control. Again, what our Parasite thinks of as right and safe is often defined by our inner five year old that didn't have the mental capacity to use reason and logic. Children were told what to believe by other's Parasites...and the idea of the sins of the fathers being visited on seven generations makes sense. And, still, it is all a big, fat, smelly pile of poop.

Awareness, and assuming complete responsibility for the thoughts and actions that create our lives, gives us back a measure of power - personal power, that is. Awareness puts us in the driver's seat. It takes our power and energy back from the Parasite, the Dream of the Planet and others by the very fact that we are aware of what we've been thinking that hasn't worked, and we can now choose to think and act in ways that we want to. We can choose what we believe (we already have, anyway). We can choose what we think (once we potty train our brains). We can stop limiting ourselves and make new choices for how we want our lives and ourselves to be, moving towards more integrity with who we are now. We can stop the lies, look them right in the face and go – ***Bullshit!***

It's really quite empowering! Are you ready for that walk now?

Pulling the Toltec Bits Together

So, to recap the Toltec teachings above: all human beings have been domesticated into their family, society, religion and culture's ideas on how to live life and what the right and wrong ways for us to be are. We took that information, added our own observations and beliefs from life's experiences, and the Parasite's Judge, Victim and Book of Laws were created and written – along with an incredibly long list of contradictions.

Our limited beliefs are reinforced by the fact that we will only see that which agrees with our Book of Law, ignoring every shred of evidence to the contrary. We select what evidence we will see and we will literally deny or not see whatever does not agree with, or support, our Parasite's ideas of what is right and wrong.

Most of our programming and selective evidence gathering is now unconscious, buried in the vagaries of memory and the past, yet fully operational in our lives today. These unconscious processes cause shame, guilt and a whole host of conflicting emotions we may not understand, yet usually feel (right before we deflect, deny or avoid them).

Increased awareness of what's really going on in our brains is a key to liberating ourselves from our Parasite's tyranny and cycle of abuse. If we can see the lies, distortions and misunderstandings - the poo - we can shift or reframe them towards the truth, creating beauty instead of more crap.

Taking responsibility back from people, events and our Parasite means that we know and accept that we are 100% responsible for our thoughts, words and deeds – and this knowledge gives us back choice, free will and our personal power. We learn to be at choice with our thoughts and lives rather than being governed by our Parasite, the Dream of the Planet and outdated rules and ideas that we no longer believe in.

That's not so hard, now is it? I think you'll find that these Toltec principals are really quite simple. I'm not saying it's easy to change, but it truly is simple in how it works.

Part II – Potty Training Your Brain

Now that we're on the same page with language, concepts and the means by which all this poo came into being – let's take a look at some issues that can show up when you start potty training your brain.

There are few humans alive who don't have the feeling that somehow they're missing something - missing the mark, missing the point, missing their dreams. They may even possess all of the outward signs of 'success' – the house, bank account, partner, career, car, clothes, kids, etc., and yet there's something 'missing'. It does not matter if you are struggling or if you appear to have it all; the part that's missing is a part of *YOU*.

David Wilcox said it beautifully: "When we lay our dreams to rest, we can get what's second best, but it's hard to get enough." Yes, when we lay down our dreams, when we settle for the status quo or someone else's ideas of who and what we should be – it's second best.

Every single one of us has compromised some part of ourselves to fit in, be loved, gain recognition or simply have some peace. Every single one of us has sold ourselves short or given up something – our truth, our ideas, our career, our childhood, our lives, our dreams or

48

our heart. Often, it was an altruistic choice for a noble cause, like children or actual survival. Sometimes we gave up our passion to maintain the peace and quiet because it doesn't matter that much anyway, right?

Wrong! Each individual compromise by itself doesn't matter so much, true. What does matter is that we rarely leave it at that. We developed our strategies, remember, and these became our habitual ways of responding. That 'don't rock the boat' agreement becomes a lifelong approach until suddenly you realize you've taken care of everyone else's needs and wants but not your own. You've shut up or given up chunks of yourself and you aren't living your whole life the way you'd envisioned it, the way you'd hoped, the way you dreamed it. Time is moving on, and you're still stuck in the 'same old same old'.

What helps you stay stuck is a real twist – you've also domesticated everyone else with your behaviors and strategies! That's right, folks! We domesticate the people around us into expecting our behaviors, our strategies and our actions/reactions - and now they expect us to stay that way. They stay the same and we stay the same and everyone stays happy - right?

It just doesn't seem to happen that way, as evidenced by the high divorce and career change rates in the United

States. When we begin to make changes in our lives, when we start to look at our poo and realize we're constipated, when the desire to *flush* becomes overwhelming – we meet resistance not only from our Parasite, but from many of the people around us.

So, understand that you've domesticated them. They like it when you take care of them. They're used to you taking charge. You're always so quiet and polite, rarely disagreeing. They're used to you letting them make all the decisions. You do as they ask. You don't make waves. They need you to be the life of the party. Get the picture?

One reason problems arise as they do in relationships (of all kinds) is that we are attracted to the masks people wear, the faces they show the world. We'll put on a mask and pretend to be strong, perfect, capable and brilliant to cover up that we feel insecure, scared and unworthy. We often develop relationships with the mask and not the real person underneath. Often, people don't know what they really want, or the pressure to conform is too great, so they put on a mask and follow the rules. The rules for men when I was growing up were that they had to be strong, work hard, provide for the family, retire and then they could relax. The rules for women were that they finished college, married a man, and took care of husband, home and their 2.5 children.

Given that we each have our own 'rules'; that we have domesticated the people around us to expect us to be the way we've always been (and vice-versa); that we've co-created new rules together; and given that none of these rules may be what we now want – it really helps to be compassionate and creative while you are unweaving it all. Developing compassion for ourselves with the work ahead, and also for those around us who may be confused or upset when we change, makes the transition from 'old you' to 'new you' a much kinder process.

To potty train your brain requires that you take the tools in the next section and actually use them. You learn to see your poo so you can then clean it up. By doing so, you stop making the same messes and choices, over and over again, expecting different results. They haven't worked, so stop! Flush! Start making different choices with your thoughts, reactions, actions and behaviors. Study yourself. Leave everyone else alone. Remember, there's your business, other's business and God's business - and you should only be concerned with your business.

Part III – Potty Training Tools

The Truth

To begin your way out of the poo it is helpful to acknowledge this truth – that you are an amazing, unique being with skills, contributions, insights and assets.

You are a gift - of and to - life. *Period.*

I understand that you might not believe me, yet resistance really is futile (and pointless and a little crazy making). I am asking you to step out on faith here until you can see this truth for yourself. Doesn't it make you happier to believe me than to believe your Parasite telling you that you're worthless, unlovable and somehow flawed? I mean...really?

Any lack of belief you may hold around your worth does not mean that what I've said is not the truth. Don't you *want* to be valued and worthy? Isn't that why we rebel, conform, save face or hold up a mask – so that we can be seen as worthy? We want it bad!

Another truth is that you can't see how amazing you are (yet) because of your domestication and beliefs. Someone *told* you that you weren't perfect because they had their own ideas of what perfect looked like. And *they* were domesticated, too! At a minimum, we are all told daily through advertising what 'perfect' looks like – the perfect job, car, house, body, soap, clothes, dishwasher and even toilet paper! Folks, it's a load of poo, and yet advertising works so well because we all desperately want to be and have "perfect".

So, please believe me when I say that you are awesome - even if you don't look like an Olympian seducer in your shiny sports car parked outside your massive mansion with your sexy spouse and stunningly beautiful 2.5 children! This isn't *who* any of us is. A car and house does not a person make – *so stop comparing yourself to others!* You have your gifts, others have theirs, and each of us is unique – so comparing ourselves to others is a waste of time and energy. It is also true that often the material 'things' we gather are a mask we wear; they're smoke and mirrors hiding our deep insecurity that we are, deep down, somehow bad or flawed.

You might be behaving and thinking in ways that limit you - but you, yourself, are a perfect, dynamic, unique and valuable gift of - and to - life. **Period**!

Thankfully, we can change our self-limiting crap. We *have* to change it. We can change how we think and how we act. We can make amends where we feel we need to.

We truly can be who we want and live a life that we've dreamed of having.

To do that, however, we have to be willing to believe in the first tool: the truth that we **are** worthy and that we deserve not only change, but the very best in life. I read a cute quote in an outhouse at the Lama Foundation once that said "God don't make no junk!" It's true. We are absolutely worthy of our birthright, which is a life *we* choose to create for ourselves.

Our choices are made via our thoughts. Thoughts are, essentially, harmless brain activity – unless and until we believe them. Thoughts, while they may be relentless, are just thoughts. The problems and 'games' began when we became attached to the thoughts we were *trained* to believe, and to those we developed on our own through life experiences. We were told until we could tell ourselves, over and over, reams of misinformation. You may have been told you weren't loveable or worthy – but it is simply not true. And, you do not have to believe it – so stop choosing to believe this crap!

Remember, too, that we are not our actions. Just because you did something dumb does not mean that you *are* dumb. Just because you made a mistake does not mean that *you* are a mistake. Just because you cheated, lied, or feared does not mean that you are a cheater, liar or weak. Period!

This truth – that you are a wondrous, valuable, unique gift of life - is the first tool to get you moving in the right direction. Keep reading on, dear one, there are lots more!

Ruthless Compassion

My teacher Raven drilled this tool into me, and it is what you want to bring to your work on yourself – ruthless compassion. You become ruthless, in that you are single-minded in your determination to clear out your crap; and you develop compassion about the fact that accepting and integrating these principals is also a process. You didn't learn to walk overnight and you won't best your Parasite overnight, either.

Please understand that *you are learning here*! You will be learning to do things you may have never done before, including being deeply compassionate with yourself. Truly, many of us have never shown ourselves the same compassion we'd show our dog, and it's time to change that behavior.

Please be compassionate with yourself and with others because *we are* all *learning here*. Bring in your wise parental controls to love on you (see next tool). Give yourself a hug, breathe and take a step back from your issues to gain a larger perspective. Be ruthless in your use of these tools, and gift yourself with compassion when it takes time to perfect both your understanding and your skill with them.

Parental Controls – New and Improved!

Many people didn't have parents that they'd like to model 'parental controls' after, so let's imagine what our ideal parents would be like.

First, they'd love us unconditionally, right? That means that no matter what we did, or how we did it, they'd still love us. We wouldn't have to be good to be loved, or make the bed to be loved, or take out the trash, or get good grades, or tell lies, or believe what they believed, or follow in their footsteps, or dumb down for them, or, or, or. Unconditionally means our ideal parents will love us *with no conditions being placed on that love* - no matter what. Sounds pretty good!

Next, ideal parents would be kind and compassionate with us, right? This means that they'd listen to us and be sympathetic. They'd understand when we messed up because everyone messes up. They'd know that we are doing our best. They wouldn't be a wicked witch or drill sergeant with us, trying to scare or drill us into submission. They wouldn't ignore us because they really do care. They'd honor that we have our lessons to learn and they'd support us through that learning.

Ideal parents would be really wise. They'd see the big picture – we're learning and growing and need all their love and support to do it. They'd also be able to gently correct our course if we're spinning out and, through love, bring us back to center – our center. They'd help us remember to use all we've learned to help ourselves. They'd help us to find our truth within us, and to navigate around any lies and distortions we might encounter.

You can add to this list, of course, but in short, ideal parents would bring all of their loving wisdom and support to hold us when we're scared, kiss the boo-boos, give us room to breathe and grow, and gently bring us back to awareness if we're about to step in front of a moving train. They want us to live – but they want us to live *our own* life.

Keeping this idea of a wise, loving parent in mind, you need to know that you can develop this amazing being inside of yourself. I say develop, because it is already there. There is already a loving, caring, unconditional part of you inside of you. Its voice may be buried under a load of poo, but it is there. You just have to cultivate it, and that takes practice.

This practice will look a lot like re-parenting yourself. This loving inner wise being is your adult self, your wise self – without all the poo. It has been rooting for you all along, you simply haven't listened. *You simply haven't listened.* Its voice might have been overshadowed by the Parasite, but it is there.

The work comes in choosing to listen. You have to choose to *know* that you are learning here, that you don't know it all yet, that your Parasite is telling you lies and distortions and that there are many things that aren't what you thought they were – including yourself and all the rules about how things are, or are supposed to be.

You have to listen to your wise parental wisdom when it tells you to cut the crap! When it says you are an amazing, blessed being – you listen to it! You make the choice not to listen to your Parasite telling you how you'll never make it because you're so unworthy and unlovable. It isn't true! You might be *acting* from your Parasite, but you, yourself, are an amazing gift of life. Remember – "God don't make no junk!"

Practice separating what you've *done* from who you *are*. You are a gift; a beautiful, precious gift from and for life. What has happened is this: you have simply done your best. You might have made mistakes, but who doesn't? You can clean up your messes and get back on track when you derail. We learn our best lessons from our mistakes – so don't ever forget that. Use your mistakes as an ally to help you find the lesson or the advantage behind every event. The lessons are there. Be willing to give yourself a break and to make different choices.

Bring in your wise Parental Controls and practice listening to them. When you make a mistake, what would your wise parent say to you? Would it slap you upside the head and call you stupid? No! It would hug you and say "try again". If you were scared, would it tell you to buck up and get over it? No! It would hold you and examine your fears to see where and if there was any truth to them. If you felt unlovable, would your loving parent laugh at you and say you're right? *NO!* It would hold you and tell you how precious you are, how beautiful and gifted and talented you are. And if you said that you weren't as smart and beautiful and successful as others, would your loving wise parent agree with you? *NO, NO, and NO!!* It would tell you how unique you are, that you have areas where you excel and that you have talents that are special to you.

And every single word of this wise parent would be *TRUE*. Period.

It's your choice, but if you're going to potty train your brain, you'll have to use parental controls. These will give you a hug when you fall, love you into getting up again and help you separate the truth from the poo. And what a lovely way to start potty training - using love and compassion!

What's Wrong With You?

If you still think I'm 'full of it', that's OK. I have a challenge for you. I want you to take some time, like a few days or a week, so that you can really give this your all. Seriously, give it everything you've got.

Here's what I want you to do: make a list of every single thing that's wrong with you. This isn't a dissertation, but a list, so write it in list form. I don't want you to write *why* you're awful, bad or wrong, just *what* is awful, bad and wrong. Don't leave anything out. No one but you will ever see your list, so give it your best shot.

My page long list had things like:

I'm not smart enough	*My nose is too big*
I'm boring	*I'm fat*
I'm not loveable	*I'm too shy*
I'm a bad dancer	*I'm lazy*

Got the idea? Great! Now get on *your* list, and later in this book I'll tell you what to do with it.

Big, Bad Pain

This is another agreement we have learned – that pain is bad. Think of all of the movies, books and TV shows that portray people sobbing from the emotional, physical and spiritual pain they've encountered. It is so horrible that they'll never love, trust, talk, try, risk, adventure, be big, be seen, be great – ever again – because it hurt...once. The message clearly says that to hurt is on par with death and destruction. Most of the time that's just poo.

Remember falling and skinning your knee? Sure, it hurt some, but what was more startling was the parent running out of the house in a panic to see if you'd killed yourself or not. I've watched parents handle falls, spills, cuts and bruises in their kids with a calm acceptance (we all fall, right?), and I noticed one amazing thing. Their kids didn't go into fits of drama around their boo-boos! They might have cried if it hurt a lot, but they didn't go into victim, scream for their parent's attention or throw a fit. In fact, it was more like, "OK, Dad....where's a Band-Aid so I can get out there and keep playing?"

We have been trained to run fast and far from *anything* that we think might hurt us – to the detriment of our very lives. You know this is true because you've seen it in yourself and everyone around you. We have been shown so many times that pain is to be avoided at all costs, that we won't take risks. We bury the emotions, buck up, shut up, shy away, outright avoid and otherwise close ourselves off from love, jobs, adventures, new friends, relationships, marriage, divorce and you name it - because it's safer that way. Sticking with the 'safe', mundane status quo is far preferable than anything that's scary, unknown and *might* cause us pain. *Even if it's the very best thing for us!*

Remember – the Parasite wants to be safe and right – no matter what! And that includes allowing you to run, hide and bury your emotions and your truth so that you sink into a dark, safe, boring, unhealthy hole. It tells you that stepping into your real truth and power is way, way too scary and unknown. Better the hole we know than risk an adventure outside where lions and tigers and bears (oh my!) might lurk to hurt us.

Joe Vitale said something that's chillingly true about this dynamic:

"When you bury an emotion, you bury it alive."

Our Book of Law, with its lies, misunderstandings, contradictions and beliefs is still inside of us, buried but still alive and operating. Our refusal to examine our pain, examine our fears and beliefs, lies and distortions, keeps us caught in a stranglehold of conflict. We may have buried it deep, but it is all still alive within us.

So, get over it. *Really*. Stop running away from everything you think might hurt you. Stop avoiding your boo-boos, poo-poo and ouches. Pain, by definition, hurts, but we're the ones that make it horrible. We're the ones that hold on tight to our pain so it can't run its course. We're the ones that make ourselves suffer, over and over again. The painful event stops, the person is gone or the event is over, and yet we keep it alive and aching inside of us. We bury it alive, and because it's still alive, we project it onto our present and our future – *where it is no longer actually happening*. Disaster mind then creates assumptions, dramas and lies to keep the pain alive.

I know it will feel counter-intuitive, but this tool says to stop running away from pain and discomfort and turn *towards* it. Bring on the lions and tigers and bears! Experience them, don't bury them. Play tantrum - close your door, take the phone off the hook, and then go through the emotion. Rant, rave, sob, scream, beat a pillow, pound the floor, break dishes – do whatever you can to let the emotion arise and be experienced. Allow your emotions to run through you *so they can run out of you.* STOP BURYING THEM ALIVE!

On the flip side of burying or ignoring pain, some people do nothing *but* focus on their sadness, faults, grief and pain. They keep them alive and clutched to their chests like a badge of honor. They feed their pain; suffering over and over and over again about events or people long since past. This, too, keeps people running away from living their life today. Their victim has them locked in the past, bringing it present, and holding on to it tightly.

There is a beautiful Cherokee legend called *Grandfather Tells* or *The Wolves Within* that illustrates our choices with what we hold on to:

An old Cherokee Grandfather is teaching his grandson about life. "A fight is going on inside of us all," he says to the boy. It is a terrible fight and it is between two wolves. One wolf is bad – he is anger, jealousy, sorrow, regret, greed, arrogance, self-pity, guilt, resentment, inferiority, lies, false pride, superiority and ego." He then says, "The other wolf is good – he is peace, love, joy, hope, serenity, humility, kindness, empathy, generosity, truth, compassion and faith. Every one of us has this same fight going on inside of us."

His young grandson thought about it for a minute and then asked his Grandfather, "Which wolf will win?" And, his Grandfather simply said, "The one you feed."

Think about this! It has been said that pain is unavoidable yet suffering is optional. We will all experience pain. We suffer, though, when we hold onto it, nurture it and define ourselves with it. That is suffering. To stop suffering, we have to stop holding on to our pain and let it go. Let go of the stories you're telling yourself and others about your pain. It doesn't mean you'll forget, but if you're tired of your suffering, you have to stop holding on to it and let it run out of you. Otherwise, you'll continue to miss the magic of life flowing around you.

With all pain, you will usually have to work at releasing it more than once. It took our lives to get to this level of constipation and it will take some time to release it all. That's OK, because you know you're learning and this isn't something you've done much of before. Play tantrum often. Get movies to stimulate your feelings. Bring in your loving parental controls. Turn towards that scared, hurt inner you and love on yourself, hold yourself, give yourself a hug, tell yourself it will be OK and that this, too, shall pass. It *will* pass, if you let it, and you *will* be OK.

Stalking

Yes, you read right – stalking. And I mean it exactly the way we usually think about it. Ever watched a cat stalk a bird or a moth? They watch its every move; they watch the paths it travels, the heights and depths it moves at. A cat will spend a long time watching its prey before it pounces, and this is the same level of concentration you need to bring to your own stalking.

Except here you're stalking yourself. Whew, huh? You thought I'd jumped off the crazy end of the pier, didn't you?

It is an incredible skill to learn to stalk yourself and become aware of the nuances of you. In this case, we're talking about stalking both your mind and your body. Humans in western cultures have developed an unfortunate reliance on the mind as our primary information gathering device. They say that mind and logic are everything, and exclude everything else. This is not only foolish, but could become humanity's downfall.

We are complex beings with many senses, all providing information to our brain. Most of that information comes in well below our conscious awareness. Parts of our awareness have been trained out of us. A fact I'd like you to verify for yourself is that our bodies will react to stimuli long before our minds realize what's going on. Our bodies will tighten to stress, relax at certain sounds, eat in unconscious situations, panic for no apparent reason and go through a whole host of reactions that we rarely pay attention to.

If I had you in my class I'd guide you through an experiment I use to help students understand where and how their bodies react to certain stimuli. I'd run through a variety of emotions expressed as sounds, and students track where in their bodies they have a reaction, and what type of reaction they have.

Examples: rage and sorrow are usually felt as a muscular tightening or closing down, whereas laughter and joy are often felt as an opening or expansion. All of these feelings/emotions are experienced in different parts of the body. Reactions are often experienced in the face, neck, shoulders, chest, and stomach, although they can be experienced anywhere.

Our bodies are incredibly sensitive (reacting to thoughts and experiences we aren't even conscious of) and they can be an amazing tool when used as such. An example from my life:

I was driving to an important event that I was presenting at, and as I drove I noticed my solar plexus had just clenched. Strange, I thought, since I couldn't identify any reason for anxiety. So I replayed (stalked) the last few minutes of what I'd been thinking, only to find that I'd tightened up when I thought of my meeting. I was completely unaware that I had any anxiety about this meeting! Once I saw this, I mentally ran though my materials and preparations and told myself that it was OK, that I was prepared and that the meeting would be fine.

I know with absolute certainty that if I had ignored the anxiety I was feeling, I would have made mistakes at that meeting. My body would have been tight and anxious, and blood wouldn't have flowed to my brain when I needed it most! By being aware and stalking my body (and then my mind), and by facing my fear, bringing in parental controls and reassuring it with the truth – that I was prepared – I avoided having that anxiety build until I was nervous and made a mistake.

Another example everyone can relate to is that of feeling someone looking at you, or watching you behind your back. You get the feeling, and turn to see a friend coming towards you or a stranger staring at you. Your body has registered something you couldn't even see.

Our bodies give us warnings, alerts and signals all the time but we usually don't listen to more than the stomach growling or the arousal in our loins. Consider the idea that most of our illnesses are a result of our not paying attention and not heeding the alerts and signals that our bodies send us. I read years ago that stress was the leading cause of cancer. It is a stunning example of the effects of relying solely on our minds, ignoring our body's wisdom and messages, and thus creating an unfortunate, unintentional reality.

It is an important tool to stalk our body and pay attention to what it has to show us, and to honor that it is trying to alert us to something our minds haven't quite figured out yet. This is why stalking our bodies is so very important. If you can accept that you are a multi-faceted being with many sources of information coming in to you, you can begin to open and explore new dimensions of both yourself and the world around you.

Stalking the mind is a bit easier, though infinitely more slippery, as this is the domain of the Parasite. The Parasite wants to be safe and right, right? So, often our Parasite goes underground with its machinations, cozy alongside all of our unconscious rules and beliefs (which is why we need the body's help to ferret things out).

To begin stalking your body, pay attention to how your body reacts to different stimuli and where in your body you sense the different emotions of anger, anxiety, stress, love, joy, sorrow, pain, shame and grief. Does your body tighten, relax, get warm, cold or tingle? Knowing how your body reacts to stimuli will become an alert to you that something is going on when your mind isn't paying attention.

With stalking your mind, simply pay attention to the thoughts that run through your head. Notice all the times you defeat yourself and have self-limiting or domesticated thoughts like: I can't, I should, I shouldn't, I'm afraid of, I'll never, it won't, I always, I'm not good enough, I hate myself, nobody loves me, nobody understands me, etc.

This is the hard part - actually seeing the poo you're thinking and (through repetition), etching permanently in your brain. Practice makes permanent, remember? Stalk your body and mind. Bring in your loving parental controls. Give yourself a hug when the poo starts. Turn toward the fear or pain and examine it, question if it is *really* true and remember that you are amazing no matter what your brain says. In the section called 'BullShit', there are tools to take this process further. Really...shovels are included and suffering is optional.

The Finger

I mentioned this tool earlier in this book, but it is such a good one that it bears repeating. What you'll notice (if you're paying attention) is that as you go through life you often focus on other people: what they're doing, how they're doing it, what they're thinking, how they're right, wrong, smart, dumb, lazy, arrogant, unfair, controlling, caretaking, dense, dishonest, careless, hurtful, and, and, and......

You're all over them, you've figured them out, and you can clearly see that they have issues. Whether that may (or may not) be true is beside the point here. When you're chewing anyone or anything else up, your Parasite has taken control of your mind and taken you out of self-awareness. You've given your power away because your focus is now on their business and not anywhere close to your own.

I'll remind you again – the only place you need your focus on is your business. Period. When you find yourself chewing on someone or something, as tempting as that might be, it is not effective in poo removal.

Like many folks, I don't like clichés, but this one really worked for me: when you find yourself pointing a finger at anyone else, there are three pointing back at you. Again, try it. Whichever finger you point, your other three fingers are pointing back at you.

Use your chewing/focusing on someone or something as a red flag of warning to pay attention to. As soon as you catch yourself, turn your attention to where it belongs – firmly on you. Use this tool to wake yourself up to what your Parasite is doing. If you do, you can stop your Parasite and reclaim control of your brain. Then *you win*, not your Parasite. I like winning, don't you!

Energy – And Why the Law of Attraction *Looks Like* it Fails

Energy is a tricky thing. Science tells us, and even Oprah has said - everything is energy. Both are sharing a truth, except that we often put on our blinders and only see the evidence we want to see. Still, *EVERYTHING* IS ENERGY! I'm talking everything, folks, not just electricity. The table is energy. The plants, air, animals, water, earth – are all made up of energy. Everything we see around us is made up of energy, including us. Cool, huh? You might be sagely thinking, "Well, duh!" about now, but have you ever considered that our thoughts are energy, too?

It is this premise, that thoughts are energy, which has fueled the Law of Attraction. As you think, you create. Every single thing in our man-made world was first a thought, an inspiration, an idea. Our thoughts, therefore, can make us sick, just as they can make us well. They can make us angry, sad, happy, jealous, agitated, rich, poor, tired, content, aggressive, worried, passive – in short, our thoughts truly create our reality. If you think something is bad, it's bad. If you change your thoughts and how you think about something, it changes. It's no longer bad. It might be inconvenient or uncomfortable, but in truth, it just *IS*. You are the one labeling it good or bad. The situation itself is just what's happening and has no meaning beyond the one you assign it. You're the one making a big deal out of it. You're the one deciding if it's good or bad, happy or sad. You're the one allowing your Parasite to chew it (and yourself) up one side and down the other. You are. No one else but you is creating your reality.

The Buddha had a wonderful teaching on this point: "What we are today comes from our thoughts of yesterday, and our present thoughts build our life of tomorrow: Our life is the creation of our mind."

When the Law of Attraction became vogue, many people began to assume responsibility for their thoughts, usually with the intention of creating something new in their lives. They'd envision themselves wealthy, having the new house/body/bank account/job/partner/etc. and they spent a lot of time using affirmations, visualization and positive thinking aimed at acquiring their new thing.

Sometimes it worked, often it didn't. I had people asking me why, when they do all the affirmations, positive thinking and visualizing, they still hadn't attracted what it was they thought they wanted in their lives?   You're probably getting the picture by now and could answer this one, but here's what I do.

I ask them if they also have thoughts that say that what they want might be scary to have, or if they still have thoughts that they shouldn't have it, or if they still feel that somewhere deep down inside that they don't deserve it. In every single answer I've ever heard (and we're talking many), the answer has been – Yes!   They still held self-limiting ideas or beliefs about themselves.

It is important to understand that *every single thought we have* has energy behind it.   The Law of Attraction works *100% OF THE TIME*.   It's not just the 'good' thoughts that are going out there and manifesting – it is every single one of them - the good, the bad and the ugly.   So, for example, if you want to attract wealth and yet you also believe that rich people are arrogant, stingy and bad - the two thoughts will compete and can cancel each other out.   If you want to attract a partner yet believe you're not attractive, what do you think your chances are?   If you want a new house, yet are scared of the mortgage or the responsibility, how's that going to play out for you?

Another way to look at it is that the Universe is simply saying 'yes'.   It says yes to everything!   How cool!   Yet again, it says yes to *EVERYTHING*. I'd like a new job. Yes! I'm not good enough for that job. Yes! I'd like to travel to Asia. Yes! I don't have enough money. Yes! I'd like to lose weight. Yes! I don't have any willpower. Yes! I'd like to work out. Yes! I'm too lazy. Yes! I'm going to be tired tomorrow. Yes! I'll get a good night's sleep. Yes!

An experience I had around sleep (which I am quite attached to) finally and deeply drilled into me the point that we create our reality. I'd been helping out at one of Don Miguel's retreats and had really long days. I was going to bed the first night and as I set my alarm I realized I'd only get six hours of sleep. My mind said, "No! I'm going to be exhausted tomorrow!" Thankfully, I caught that thought and realized what I was doing. I was setting myself up for a really bad day simply by how I was thinking about it. So, I said instead, "I'm going to get a good night's sleep and wake up feeling great." I woke up the next day refreshed and had a great day. The second night, setting my alarm and seeing I'd only get six hours of sleep – *again* – my mind said, "Oh no, there's no way I'll make it through tomorrow. I'll be exhausted for sure now." Again, I caught it and again I said no, I'll sleep well and wake up rested. I had a great second day. As I went to sleep that third night, the tyrant that is my mind said exactly the same thing with even **more** feeling. I caught it and (again) changed how I thought about it. And, you guessed it, I had a great day. That had NEVER happened to me before! I had never, ever gone three nights in a row (heck, not even two) with only six hours sleep and not been tired and bitchy the next day.

That experience convinced me that we truly create our reality. The Universe is simply saying yes, folks! To everything we think. What an amazingly creative and cooperative Universe we live in. Yes!

All of these conflicting beliefs are another example of cognitive dissonance. You want something, yet you don't believe you're good enough to have it. You decide life will be a certain way (the usual, old way) you're your Parasite reinforces the status quo. This can result in delays, hassles, lessening what you attract or even prevent you from acquiring it. It can be frustrating and crazy making, but you will attract what you really think, and what you think you deserve.

This is why the Toltec path is so very effective. You can't change what you can't see, and once you learn to actually *see* what's running around your brain, you can change it. If your thoughts are energy, where do you want to put them, what thoughts do you choose to think? Do you want to reinforce the crap your Parasite tells you, or reinforce what I am telling you – that you can choose your thoughts and that you are a unique gift of life, deserving the very best?

BullShit!

This is one of my favorite poo busters because it involves bringing in the truth.

This tool is really quite simple. Since you have been stalking your mind, increasing your awareness and seeing all of the really crappy thoughts your judge and victim keep throwing at you (every minute, hour and day, if you're honest), you are now ready for another tool to stop them - *because you can now see them.*

Remember, practice makes permanent. This tool stops the thoughts from going down their old, well-worn pathways in your brain while creating new thoughts with new pathways for them to travel. You just have to actually use it.

This process involves using a powerful, 'cutting' word to first stop the crappy thought dead in its tracks. As soon as you become aware of it, you stop it. 'Bullshit' works great for me because I can say it with *lots* of energy behind it ('*Oh, bullshit!*'), but you can use any word that has power and energy for you. Some use 'cancel', 'no', 'full stop', 'error', 'terminate', 'gotcha'. It doesn't matter what the word is, as long as you use it with enough force to stop your crappy thoughts dead in their tracks.

Once you've stopped it, you then replace it with the truth, which creates a new pathway for your new thoughts to go down. Simple, yes? I know a lot of folks say to use positive affirmations and 'fake it till you make it', but that can take a long time! Positive affirmations can work, but sometimes our mind balks when told something it patently does not yet believe.

The trick is to replace the lie or distortion with the truth. Our minds have a much harder time arguing with us when we're telling it the truth. Make it a positive truth, though. Our judge can come up with a million negatives about us, so bring in your wise, creative, parental control self and create positive truths to counter them. They can be simple, just keep in mind that whatever you choose, if you repeat it enough, then *that* will become etched in your brain. (Which is why affirmations can work over time.) So, make the choice to etch in the positive – because the positive is *always* there – even if it is simply that you learned something.

Here are some simple truths I've used very successfully in response to negative thoughts: "It doesn't have to be that way", "I'm learning" and "It's a lie". That last one can take a little more convincing at first, but it's usually the truth.

Some examples of what this looks like are:

(You're going to mess up that meeting.) *GOTCHA!* That's a lie - I'm prepared and I'll be fine.

(You made mistakes, you're a failure.) *CANCEL!* I did my best, and mistakes are OK because I'm learning.

(You'll never get published.) *ERROR!* It doesn't have to be that way – of course I can be published!

(That eighteen wheeler is going to kill you.) *OH BULL!* I'm perfectly safe. (Be gone disaster mind!)

(Your friends don't really care about you.) *TERMINATE* that lie! My friends love me (I'm just tired).

(You're too overweight to date.) *STOP IT!* That's a lie, overweight people go on dates!

"It doesn't have to be that way", "that's a lie" and "I'm learning" have been my saving graces, because they are all true. Things *don't* have to be the way my disaster mind, victim and judge say they will be. Much of what my mind tells me really *is* a lie, and I am most certainly learning here.

When we no longer *have* to be perfect or right, when we stop our judge and victim's tyranny, when we let go of our limiting ideas and just be us - all of who we are - the truth comes easily and we begin to taste freedom from our Parasite. So, let go of the domestication that's defining what 'perfect' means, is or looks like. Perfect is an illusion because it is different for every single person alive! It's all a dream - and you can choose your own!

Quit Holding On To Your Poo

That's right – stop it! So many hold onto, defend, justify, rationalize and absolutely refuse to let go of their poo, it's amazing. We've all heard it, someone telling us exactly why they have to be as down-trodden, defeated and dysfunctional as they are. I mean…really? Talk about self-limiting!

I call this behavior 'suffering over your suffering'. So many people actually argue for their limitations. They repeat to themselves and others: I can't do this or I'm the way I am because I'm so terrible at it and it will never change because my doctors/teachers/parents/God say I have every problem under the sun, and of course that's terribly debilitating so I'm confused and hurting and don't even know how to change or what that would look like so I'll make the best of this terrible situation, even though it stinks, but at least I know that stink and I will, somehow, handle it because this is my fate.

OK….a bit dramatic, but do you get the picture? Again, pain is inevitable, but suffering is optional. Think about it. All of us encounter conditions that are challenging, but we suffer when we think of it as suffering and especially when we suffer over our suffering! Every single time we say that we are broken or defective or that we can't do something, we are etching a pathway deeper into our brains and it becomes our reality because we believe it and *we repeat it all the time!* We hold onto it, nurture it, feed it and identify with it.

Remember, as we think, we create! There is very little that is impossible, folks, and you are going to have to let go of your attachment to your poo and suffering if you ever hope to live in freedom. Stop holding on to your 'defects'. Stop moaning over your alleged inabilities. Stop repeating, over and over - I can't, I'll never, I shouldn't, I don't – and start to at least say – I can, I will or I'm willing…to try, to experiment, to learn, to grow, to play with it and to give it a shot.

That's all I'm asking of you – to be willing to try.

Punctuate!

HeatherAsh taught me this tool, and it's a great one. I've been using it throughout this book. It's the "period". Our Parasite loves to feed us long, run together sentences:

I just made a mistake at work and now my boss will think I'm a failure just like my Daddy thought I was a failure because I can't do anything right and when I get nervous it gets even worse and my boss makes me nervous all the time because I'm sure she's watching my every move and half of those are awful and I'm just stupid because I forget to use my tools and breathe and, and, and.

Learning to punctuate is as simple as placing the period. I just made a mistake at work – PERIOD! I got nervous – period. I forgot to use my tools – period. You don't allow the judge its soap-box - period! None of these makes you a bad person. All you did was get nervous and forget to use your tools or you made a mistake or it was an accident. That's *all*.

Punctuating stops your judge in its tracks and stops your mind from running on and on. As soon as you catch a run-on guilt trip careening through your mind – punctuate! As soon as you hear your victim going off on someone – punctuate! Stop the merry-go-round, cancel the pity party, call in parental controls and punctuate. Welcome to the human race and, oh, by the way, we all have run-away brains and we're all learning here. *Period!*

What Hal Showed Me

Hal was my marriage counselor and the person who took me through the exercise of making a list of 'what's wrong with you' that I asked you to do earlier. So, please, pull out your list and a pen or pencil before you read further. It won't work if you don't grab your list and a pen, so don't ruin it for yourself, OK?

Now, imagine that you've handed me your list. You're nervous as I look it over carefully, reading every line, every single thing that's wrong with you. I'm serious, nodding my head as I say, "That's quite a list. I can see you gave it a lot of thought." I hand the list back to you. I hand you the pen. "Now, I want you to imagine your best friend, and that this is your best friend's list. Read the list carefully and put a check mark by every item on this list that you wouldn't forgive in your best friend."

Pick up your list. Read it, every line. Put a check mark by every item that you wouldn't forgive in your best friend. Really, read your list. I'll wait. And when you're finished, continue here.

There aren't any check marks, are there. And that's not a question, it's a statement, because I have never had anyone choose something that they wouldn't forgive in their best friend. Never.

Of course, you can be a prissy knit-picker and your mind can rebel and rationalize out something you wouldn't forgive, but the truth is, we are far harder on ourselves than we are on anyone else. We will usually forgive everyone else, yet not ourselves, for doing the very same actions. So, the real question is: if you would forgive your best friend, will you now forgive yourself? Please? Aren't you just as deserving of compassion and forgiveness as everyone else? Can't you understand that you were trying your best, with what tools and insights you had available at the time? Don't we all make mistakes, get scared or make bad choices? Aren't we all learning here?

You have been doing your best all of your life, and most of what's happened to you or that you've done has been a result of domestication, misunderstanding, accidents and mistakes. Period. It is time to forgive yourself.

Forgiveness has to start with us for it to extend to others. If we can bring in loving parental controls and compassion for our confusion, compassion for our fears, compassion for places we've acted from fear or times we've fallen and made mistakes – we can not only heal ourselves, but also our relationships and maybe the world. Forgiveness is such a simple yet profound tool. We start with forgiving ourselves.

Going Out of Your Mind

Yay! This is what we strive for! And it doesn't mean you check your intelligence at the door.

Our minds are, after all, the crux of most of our difficulties, so getting out of your mind is a good thing. I remember the Bible saying that it is only as little children that we can approach heaven; that we need to become as little children. In a way, that is what potty training our brains also requires – that we flush the poo we've learned and return to the magic of wonder and curiosity that children have.

In order for us to do this, to find ourselves 'not guilty' of our judgments, we must literally go out of our minds – our egoist, parasitic, domesticated minds. We have to un-learn our years of training because this is what is naming us guilty. We have to let go of all the cherished ideas we learned from everyone else that are not our truth. We have to question *every single idea we have* to understand whether it is ours - or not.

No one can judge you and find you guilty unless you agree with them. Period.

My parents and society told me it was a *SIN* to love the one I was with. Today, my truth is to love anyone I want as long as I'm within my own integrity and not hurting another soul – including myself. (And in case you didn't know this, love does not have to mean sex!)

Questioning everything takes some effort, certainly, though not as much as you might think. In fact, I bet you'll find that by simply reading the ideas and practices here, your mind has already begun to question. You've already begun to retrain your brain. You're already going out of your old, conditioned mind.

Once we gain even a little bit of awareness, we start to regain control in the form of choice. Once we see what our brain is telling us, we are at choice as to whether we travel that oft followed pathway – or whether we place our hands on the handle of the commode and – *flush!* Then create a new pathway, a new mind.

Really, 'cut the crap' and 'down the toilet' take on whole new parameters! What do *YOU* believe? What does *YOUR* heart say is true? What is it *YOU* want to do, think, be, say, wear, explore and experiment with? **What?**

Create! Invent! Play! Experiment! Become as children through the wonder of adventure! This tool says to have fun with changing your thoughts! Leave your old, crappy mind behind and create something wonderful and new for you.

Telling the Difference Between Poo and Truth

I am often asked how we can learn to tell the difference between our mind (with the crap it tells us) and, well, intuition, higher self, divine guidance, inner truth or whatever you want to call that deep, quiet 'knowing' inside that we all have.

It is true that our mind gets engaged when things come to/through us....but it is not true that everything that crosses our minds comes from our minds. That's an important distinction. Intuition, inner knowing, divine guidance, telepathy/ESP, energy - all of these things (and more) can and do come to us. Sometimes they arrive as a feeling, a sense or a knowing. Sometimes they jet straight into our brains as a thought.

When these messages arrive, our minds do register the 'arrival', shall we say. You've got mail! This new awareness does not mean that the idea, sense, knowing or feeling originated in our minds. Still, our minds will try to make 'sense' of what has arisen. Mind will try to figure it out, and will often run through all the possibilities it has stored as options to try to make things fit into a recognizable box.

The problem with this process, however, is that our minds have been selective-evidence gathering all our lives

- the stress being on selective. Our minds have vetoed anything that doesn't fit into our belief structure around what's possible, real, desirable or aversive, so it will tend to try and sort information according to its neural pathways – or ignore it as inconsequential or too strange to be true.

The trick for all of us lies in understanding what is mind - and what is intuition, higher self, inner knowing or extra-sensory information. Since we humans have developed a dangerous reliance on our minds for everything, we tend to ignore the information-gathering intelligence of our bodies and other senses. Learning to feel your body and to understand its signals (see *Stalking*) is critical in re-wiring and re-directing the mind's addiction to running our show.

Having said that, please understand that our feelings are not always reliable indicators of the truth, either. If you were traumatized as a child around water, you'll become terrified and your body will freak out if you get near large bodies of water. For example, I have a friend who panics when going over bridges. Her fear is happening despite there being *no evidence* to indicate that there is a problem with the bridge *or* the water, and yet the fear is screaming its head off.

Our work is to identify the selective evidence we've gathered that is affecting our lives today so that we can separate the truth from the lies of our domestication and programming. If you think about it, all our intuition and inner guidance have to work with is our bodies and minds - so they come in through those vehicles - but are not from those vehicles.

One tool to making this distinction between mind and intuition I learned from Buddhist teacher, Adyashanti. It shows how to separate or understand what is your intuition (inner guidance, spirit, heart), versus what is your mind, or mental thought processes:

The difference between intuition and mind is that intuition doesn't explain itself.

It's true, so pay attention to this tool! I stalked it for months before teaching this one, and found it to be true in every instance. Intuition, divine guidance, our heart's desire or inner knowing...simply come in. There's a sense, a knowing, or an awareness - *and that's it* – there's nothing more than that. Mind, however, explains every single detail, providing photos and graphs and reasons and logic. Intuition is very quiet. Mind is like Mardi Gras in New Orleans.

This is one incredibly helpful tool, and once you see your quiet inner guidance arising – do not ignore it! Please! This guidance is pointing you to your truth, so start to act on it. Follow your heart, your inner knowing and wisdom to see where it takes you – even if your Parasite is screaming at you to stop. Heck, *especially* if your Parasite is screaming at you to stop! *Your Parasite's alarm is often a clue that you should do exactly what it is explaining you shouldn't do!* Think about it. Your parasite wants you to be safe as your five year old self defined safety – but is that reasonable at twenty, thirty or sixty?

Can You Really Know?

The truth is that there are times when we are completely certain that we know what someone else is thinking or doing, or what the truth is of a situation. After all, we've had *years* of experience with these people or events and we've 'seen it all' before. When Mom gets frustrated she always gets 'The Look'. When he won't answer his phone, he's mad and avoiding me. When the boss gets 'The Look', someone's head is going to roll. When my brother/father/friend behaves that way, he's hiding something. When people cry, it's because they're sad. When she gets chatty, she's nervous about something, and that's usually me.

There are also people that have higher than average levels of empathy or telepathy, and some have learned to pay more attention to the details of what's going on than others have. Many people have learned to pick up on subtle cues, clues or 'tells' in their families and friends in order to survive. It's like having a personal radar that's scanning the environment in order to sense danger before it hits.

In these cases, we will argue that we are right, that our assessment is true and that we clearly know what's going on with the other person. We'll change our behaviors accordingly, adapting and responding to what we *think* is happening – whether it is or not. Disaster mind loves this playground, too. It will create dramatic stories about what they're thinking, what's about to happen and how wrong or weird they are being based on information that may, or may not, be true.

I'm not saying that we can't read or scan people or situations accurately at times. Of course we can. Of course we have experience that supports our mind thinking someone is mad at us. The problem, however, is that we're not 100% accurate. We might be wrong (yet we usually assume we're right), and then **we act on our assumptions!**

Here's a story to illustrate this point: I was tested in grade school for telepathy and tested much higher than average. Over time, I learned to trust this extra sense but, being the skeptic that I am, I tested it. For a solid year I kept track of every time my insight was accurate, and when it wasn't. At the end of the year, I found that 80% of the time I was accurate and 20% of the time I was completely off base. Many years later, when I hit my Toltec studies, I was still relying on my 80/20 rule. Raven tried to tell me that I couldn't possibly *know* and I rebelled because...I *knew*. Still, I agreed to run the test again, and came out with the same percentage.

Through that second year of tallying, however, I began to realize what he was trying to show me – which was that I could not absolutely *know.* It turns out he was right. As I stalked it all again, I came to understand that just because I was correct more often than not – I never, *ever* knew when that 20% was going to arise. **NEVER.** Eighty percent of the time I was right – but twenty percent of the time I wasn't – and I never, ever knew when that twenty percent would kick in. So - I never really *knew.*

You don't know, either. Sure, you'll be right some of the time, and you'll be wrong the rest of the time. The problem comes when we believe that we are absolutely right. This is a trap, folks! And it's not fair to the people in our lives when we hold on to our self-importance and insist we're right and they're wrong. It's W.A.R. all over again.

So, when this situation arises for you, as I know it will, the gift you can give yourself and others is to check out your impression. Don't assume they're thinking/being what you think they are – ask them! Talk to your people! Run your own experiment and find out how often you're right and wrong. Ask your people, get the numbers, and see what your percentages are. And, once you know that, it still doesn't matter. I now *know* that I don't know, which means that I am open to being wrong, and I am open to communicating with the people in my life rather than judging them and making assumptions. Isn't this a cleaner and more honest approach to start with?

Habit – A Slow Death

Ah…habits. We have so many of them and they are, truly, powerful sedatives and the death of wonder, curiosity and magic. Habits are a trap. They blind us to the world around us. They put us on the automatic pilot of a rote and mundane existence.

And yet, we cherish them! How many of you simply can't start your day without your cup of coffee? Tea? Newspaper? Internet? Facebook, for crap's sake? How many take the same route to work or school every single day? How many get that absentminded kiss as they head out the door?

I mean it - habits blind us to the world around us. Did you see the sunrise as you ran for the coffee pot? Did you feel the texture of the lips kissing you as you ran out the door? Did you notice the sky and air and earth as you drove to work? Did you look at the world around you as you hustled to your meeting, school or grocery store? Probably not. There is an amazing, delicious world happening all around us that habits blind us to simply because of their nature as rote, repeated actions.

One way to practice finding your truth and opening your awareness is to start to change your habits. Take the blinders off. I regularly change my schedules and habits to see the world with fresh eyes. Drive or walk a different way than usual to your destinations and see what's going on and what changes are taking place. Break up your routines so that you actually begin to see what's happening in the world around you. As you awaken, relish that kiss, glance, handshake, sunrise, forest, flower and cup of coffee.

When you do, how do you feel? The blindness to our actions causes blindness to our feelings and to the miracles of life all around us. When we go on automatic pilot, the mindlessness not only affects what we are doing, it also limits what we are feeling, being and seeing. As much as possible, bring in awareness to break your routines – and then pay attention to what you are feeling, your thoughts, how your body responds and what's new around you.

Really, this tool says to break your habits, open your eyes, open your heart and *LOOK UP!* Look around! You just might see that next opportunity, person, goal, answer, path, miracle or magical coincidence that's been there for you all along.

Southern Friendly

I grew up in the south and noticed a phenomena I came to call 'Southern Friendly'. This is where everyone has the same friendly answer to 'how are you'. They all say, "Fine, how are you?", or some version of that - no matter what. No matter how they feel or whether their dog just died...they're fine.

This automatic response used to drive me crazy because it felt shallow and is often so untrue that it deserved a label! It is another way the Parasite keeps itself safe by hiding the truth of how we're feeling and what we're doing. If we're exhausted or having a hard time, then God forbid anyone see it! We're supposed to be perfect, strong and upright, right?

So, we put on a 'fine face', a mask, so people will not see that we're hurting or scared or upset inside. We believe that it is not OK to be all that we are, the good and the sad, the beautiful and the not so cute. We believe we'll be rejected if we show up simply as we are. We've spent years selectively gathering evidence to support this notion – but having done so does not mean that it is true.

Where in your life can you take off the mask and simply be you, even just a little? When someone asks how you're doing today, try saying 'Great!' or 'Not so great today' or 'Boy, am I tired'. In the section below I talk more about masks, and the section on running experiments includes tools to help you un-mask.

Being Seen - or - Look at this Pretty Mask!

Authenticity is what everyone is truly afraid of. We are terrified of actually being seen. If you think about it, from the Dream of the Planet's perspective, this fear makes sense. If we believe that we're somehow broken, weak, vulnerable, incompetent, bad, unworthy and unlovable – the last thing we want is for everyone else to see it, too! I mean, *SHIT!*

So, everyone with an out of control Parasite (which is most folks) is running around thinking the same thing, and doing the same thing – holding up a mask to deflect and distract attention in order to hide. I can't let them see how weak or scared I am, so let me give them something else to focus on. There, again, is the Parasite telling us what we *should* be, do and look like. Behold the birth of our masks. Any time we tell ourselves that we don't measure up, we put on a mask and fake it.

Ancient Toltecs were great mask-makers because they saw what humans were doing, and they used masks to illustrate their awareness. They understood that we hold up a mask so people will see it, and not see what we think are our flaws and fears beneath it.

There are as many masks as there are people, and we each have many of them for the various situations in our lives. There's the I'm patient mask, I'm competent mask, I'm weak mask (so please help me), the innocent child mask, the mother, father, single, hustler, hooker, aristocrat, poor me, teacher, student, athlete, etcetera masks. Whew! Hundreds of them!

The challenging part of our mask addiction is that our masks have come in handy and have saved us many times – even though they are not the truth. We've all experienced situations where a mask really helped us to *look* strong, competent, weak, aggressive, etc. Many men put on a macho, cute or seductive mask to approach women. People often put on an unemotional mask at work. It is often said among women that we have to put on a 'don't mess with me' mask when we approach auto mechanics so we look like we're on the ball and they don't take advantage of us. Or, we put on the 'I'm helpless' mask so the hero can ride to our rescue, saving the damsel in distress.

Problems arise, however, when we begin to identify with our masks or when, as in the movie 'The Mask' with Jim Carey, they get glued to our face and we can't take them off. We develop the habit of presenting our masks to the world, rather than our true selves.

The belief that we have to be seen a certain way to be accepted arises from our insecurities learned through domestication and our Book of Law. Remember, so much of our domestication is a lie. Yet, people marry these masks, hire these masks and make friends with these masks. It takes tremendous energy and stress to keep the masks in place, and eventually we get tired, stressed, in a hurry or fed up and we slip. People see behind the mask; they see a part of us we've been hiding. We really *are* angry, we're tired of being compliant, we don't like things, we're really not that passive or strong or brave, etc. At times, taking off our masks results in divorce, the loss of a job or a friendship – but *only* because we've been hiding our truth and essentially lying all along.

Wearing our masks often becomes a habit, and when we're stuck in habits we've not only blinded ourselves, but we've lost or forgotten our ability to choose. Thinking we don't have a choice means we've given our personal power away to someone or something outside of us. We are out of control – of ourselves. When this happens, when we give our power away to others, everyone has the ability to ruin our day, rain on our parade, make us mad and essentially determine our self worth because we gave them the power to do so. By not being honest, by not being ourselves or making our own choices, we've given others power over us.

The point is not that we'll never put on a mask again. Skill with masks can be really helpful at times, which is why we started using them in the first place. The point, however, is to be in awareness and choice versus habit and domestication. You are always making choices, remember? You can choose to put on a mask now and then if it will (really) serve you best. But watch out for habitual mask wearing. Just because you've always done it, it doesn't mean it's good for you or that you have to.

To get out of the habit of wearing your masks will require you to let it slip now and then, if not toss it out altogether. (Gulp!) Start practicing with friends, partners and trusted people in your life. Start small. I started playing with this dynamic by running experiments to see if I could collect different evidence. I mean, I was *told* it was worth letting my masks go, but I had to experience something different to actually *know* it.

Running Experiments

To understand that the world isn't what we think it is, we need to collect new evidence. We've been selectively gathering evidence to support our limiting beliefs all of our lives, and we need new evidence to support changing them. Running experiments is a good way to start. I say *experiments* here so that the mind doesn't panic and think it might actually have to change forever and so stops you dead in your tracks!

You see, our Parasites need some convincing that it's safe to let go. Here's an example:

I am a really competent person. I've had years of widely varied experiences in many different areas and like to say I've gone from barns to boardrooms and everywhere in-between, which is pretty much true. Yet, I'd use my 'I'm competent mask' so that people would do things my way. After all, I really *was* competent and usually *did* know a good way to get a job done, but I became identified with my mask. I controlled everything. Jobs got done – by me. Frankly, it was exhausting.

So, HeatherAsh gave me an experiment to run. I was then the Finance Director of a non-profit and I was running a large community program involving lots of meetings. She told me that for the next month, my experiment was to not run *any* meeting. None, zero - period. I balked! I told her it was impossible, and she smirked at me. She *smirked!* I was really committed to my freedom, though, so I (very) reluctantly agreed to try.

To my complete and utter amazement, it was great! People began to step up and take on tasks. The burden of this huge program began to be shared among others involved. My work load decreased. People rose to the occasion and were able to express their own talents and skills. It wasn't all done the way I'd do it, but it all got done and some of it better than I'd imagined.

Here are some clues to running your own experiments – whatever you usually do – don't. And you don't run the experiment with vindictiveness or spite or let your Parasite try to make it fail. If there's something you're afraid of – do it (gulp!). I didn't like heights, so did a zip line. I was terrified the first three trees – then I loved it!

If you're usually quiet, start speaking up more. If you usually control, then back off and let others take the lead. If you usually talk first, shut up for a change. If you usually lie and say you're fine, try saying you're stressed or tired or whatever is going on. If you never talk to strangers, try asking the grocery clerks how they're doing. If you never share your personal feelings, choose a friend to open up with….and then watch the results.

Keep a rein on your Parasite, folks, so it doesn't set up self-defeating situations! Don't start with the Mt. Everest of the hardest and scariest experiments to run. The point is to succeed, so start with baby steps, running experiments with people you know and trust a bit (or don't know at all!). You can even tell people you're running an experiment if that makes it easier. Maybe they'll support you and hold your hand. The point is to run the experiment to see what you might learn about yourself and your preconceived ideas if you didn't do what you've always done, or if you do what you've always avoided. Open to the possibility that your closely held ideas and beliefs might be wrong, and collect the evidence to support that. Being wrong is great! *What a relief!*

And yes, straight up – some experiments are scary. That's OK. I was TERRIFIED when I started that zip line. When you're scared, bring in parental controls. Your loving, wise parent self *knows* you can do this and it has the bigger picture. Your Parasite says you're going to *die* if you talk to that person, and your wise self knows it's not true - you'll live. Parasite says you *have* to take care of everyone else; wise self says stop and see, because you might actually empower them instead. Parasite says it's too scary to share; wise self knows that folks have wondered why you haven't.

Fear is the first gateway we all have to walk through so that we can collect new evidence in our lives, and fear stops most people from ever doing that. How many times has fear stopped you from doing something? Really, think about this. We could all make quite a list, I'm sure. Remember, though, that our fears are not necessarily true. You might *believe* that it's true, but that doesn't mean it is. Question EVERYTHING!

I've done all these things, and more, and can honestly say that I've been badly received maybe once...by someone I didn't know very well and who was probably having a bad day. In the end, it didn't matter that they weren't receptive to me because I wasn't doing it for them – I was doing it for me. Furthermore, I didn't let my Parasite have a field day with their rejection. It was one time among many more times where I was received with understanding, compassion and love.

People *yearn* for honest relationships. People *yearn* for someone else to open the door by being honest so that they can be honest, too. People *yearn* for something more than the rote, mundane, boring excuse we often have for interactions. *You yearn* to let go and just be who you are. I'm telling you, you're amazing, so try running experiments so you can learn that it really is OK to be you.

Some experiments you run will require your behavior to change, and the changes won't go unnoticed. After all, you've always been the way you were, so people will probably wonder what's up. If someone asks if you're feeling OK today, just smile and say you're running an experiment, trying to gain some new insights into your habits. It's really easy!

I'm Gonna Blow!

Since we haven't been exactly honest with ourselves and others, stuffing ourselves into somebody's idea of what we should be like and burying most of our emotions alive...well...pressure has built up. When the pressure gets intense enough, there is a tendency for people to 'blow'. We've all seen this happen and most of us have experienced it – the last straw, the end of our rope, the letting off of steam.

It usually makes us feel better, too, right before the guilt and shame kick in that we've just yelled at our kids, pet, boss, employee, partner, friend or stranger. Then we feel awful again.

The key here is to look at what created the pressure in the first place. We've got to stop stuffing, folks! We have to stop burying our truth alive and accept that we're human and humans have emotions. Really, it's OK. It isn't that our emotions are bad – it's what we do with them that hurts the most.

When we vent our emotions on other people, spreading our poo and poison everywhere, we hurt and poison them. When we bury and stuff them inside of us, we hurt and poison ourselves. Nobody wins in either of these scenarios, and so much harm is done that simply isn't necessary. I understand that it's how we've been trained, but it's killing us. So, stop it.

Buddhist mindfulness meditation is great for gaining awareness of the arising, existing and passing away of thoughts and emotions. If you stalk yourself closely, you'll see the same thing. Thoughts and feelings arise, and if we let them exist and run their course, they also pass away. It's the passing away we're shooting for here. It's when we stuff and bury these thoughts and feelings that problems arise.

Practice experiencing and releasing thoughts and emotions instead of holding on, bucking up, being stoic, or a martyr or saving face. Again, play tantrum to let the feelings flow through and out of you. Speak your truth.

You don't have to yell it at the top of your lungs. It is quite acceptable to say, 'You know, I'm getting frustrated, confused, angry, hurt here' – BEFORE you're really ticked off and yelling or throwing things. Take a walk to gain some space from the irritation. Say you need a break to collect yourself or take a potty break.

Once you've created physical space or distance, do everything you can to vent off some steam and emotions. Turn towards it, acknowledge how you feel, then let the feeling flow and be expressed so it doesn't get stuck inside of you. Breathe deeply, give a primal yell or a silent scream, cry, shake your body all over to release pent up energy, jog in place – *do something* to help the energy of the emotion to be released from your body.

This releasing can sometimes feel really, really scary to do. Contrary to all logic, I used to feel that if I really vented my anger, I'd run amok and destroy the world. This fear kept me burying my anger, over and over again. It took a number of times of really going for it, of beating the crap out of a pillow or my woodpile or the ground (when no one could hear me or interrupt), for me to finally vent off enough anger that I could handle it when it arose around others. With sadness and grief, I cried an ocean of tears before the pain finally lessened enough for me to be able to handle it easily.

Emotions will pass away, if we let them; flowing out like a stream. Our Parasite often has other ideas, though. Weird as it sounds, we often find our pain and suffering to be safe and familiar, like an old shoe we should have thrown out years ago but didn't. This is yet another case of – STOP IT! You either stop burying and stuffing now, or you wait until you are so sick and tired of the pain that you can't stand it anymore – or that heart attack wakes you up – or your partner leaves you – or you destroy yourself with drugs, alcohol or loneliness. What a waste that would be of the precious gift of life that you are!

Empty Gas Tank

Another thing humans do is focus on empty. Cars have a meter that tells us when the tank is full or empty, and empty is usually a bright red line, easy to see.

In life, when the shit hits the fan or we're 'up to our eyeballs in it', all we can focus on is that one, red, empty line. It sucks us in so that all we see are our faults, our imperfections, our pain and our fears. It draws our attention to lack, to less, to fear, to judgment – and it's just a line! Yet, we become totally absorbed in this one aspect of the tank, ignoring the rest of it.

Here's a head's up - we're full tanks, folks! We're dynamic, multi-faceted, complex beings, and it is a crime to define ourselves by that one red line. Just because it's easy to see doesn't mean the rest of the tank doesn't exist.

When you find yourself focusing on that empty red line, bring in the truth and remember that you are more than that line. Bring in the truth, but bring all of it in. When you focus on your faults, never forget your virtues, because they are there, too.

There's a whole tank waiting for you to notice. Sure, you might have made a mistake. It's true that you don't know it all yet. Of course you haven't fixed every single thing in your life. So what? You've learned, you've grown, and you are far vaster than all of it. You have skills and insights and gifts and beauty that add up to a whole tank just waiting for you to stop your pity party and suffering over your suffering. It's true!

My support is that you do an *honest* inventory of your life's successes (and only successes), using your heart's weights and measurements. I did this once, and was astounded. Like you, I'd only focused on empty, and it was an eye opening exercise to see all the places I hadn't failed – the big ones and the small. I included items like these: That I helped people, that I was good at batik, that I was honest and that I was learning and facing my fears. These are successes, too, beyond passing a test, reaching goals or getting a job.

Make your own success inventory. Truly honor and acknowledge *all* of your successes, big and small, and use your own standards to measure them by – and no one else's. Let the 'shoulds' go. Let your parent's, teacher's, society's, kid's and partner's ideas of what you should be and do go. Heck, let your own 'shoulds' go, too! If you do, I bet you'll be just as astounded as I was because you're just like me – human, unique and possessing a whole host of gifts. We are all a full tank, folks, so just open your eyes and see it; bookmark your strengths, remember all of you when that empty red line looms large in your vision. It's just a line, and a small one at that!

Black and White

'Black and White' is a fixation method our Parasite uses to take us out. It's along the lines of 'either/or' and 'all/or nothing'. With the empty tank, you're focused only on your faults. With black and white, you're torn between opposites - usually extreme opposites.

Black and white can look like: you either have to leave her, or stay unhappily with her; you either take the job or stay home with your kids; you either completely focus or completely let go; you either do one thing, or you stay stuck in the another thing. Black and white is rarely true.

There are other options if you expand the 'box' of how you are thinking about it. There are other colors!

When we've hit black and white, we're usually in emotional constipation or upheaval. Nothing is working out the way we'd hoped, and our options appear limited. The point here is that we're experiencing an upheaval, and that isn't the greatest place to make decisions from, at least not on our own. It is also not a place to get advice from people that are strongly opinionated about our upheaval. They could have an agenda, or their own motivations, as to what they'd like for us to do.

When you hit black or white, you need blood flowing to your brain, so the first thing to do is to breathe and try to relax. Next, take a big step back - away from the problem - so that you can look at it from different angles. Bring in your creative parental controls and see what they have to say. Bring in some humor and create as many *other* options (especially silly, crazy ones) that you can think of. Doing so will coax your mind to edge out of the box you've created around the problem. If you aren't gaining new perspectives, go to an unbiased friend and ask him or her to help you create and explore new options.

A woman at a workshop shared her problem of not finding a partner, adding that she had pretty much given up trying. Partnering with another participant, they brainstormed as many *other* options to giving up as they could: go on a dating website, join outdoor activities groups, start looking men in the eyes, volunteer at the Army Navy store....and her hilarious 'crazy' one: run naked through the park with her phone number written on her back! Now, *that's* thinking outside the box!

There are *always* other options if we take a breath and look for them. Situations are not black and white, and the same can be said for almost everything in life.   Our Parasite and domestication may say otherwise, but there are a lot of colors, there's middle ground, and there's a wide, glorious gulf to explore between black and white.

Back-Tracking

Back-tracking is a tool that your Parasite will *HATE*. It will hate it so much, in fact, that we can often eliminate a lot of poop by simply *threatening* to back-track.

The concept is simple. If you mess up, you fess up. That's right, fess up. You're gaining an appreciation of the fact that you're learning here, and just like the rest of us, mistakes get made, our strategies raise their heads or we put the mask back on. We may have regressed, or made a boo-boo, but remember - our mistakes are not us! Since we aren't our mistakes, it's really simple to go back and fix them.

Fixing our mistakes can look like:

You know when I said I like Italian food, I was only trying to please you because I actually hate it, or

I know I said that I could finish fast, but it's taking more time than I thought, or

I didn't tell you the whole truth because I was afraid you would leave me, or

I didn't speak up because I didn't know what to say, or

I told you I could help you but I realized that I desperately need a day off, or

I messed up and I'm sorry, or

I was too scared, or..........

Start out simply, with smaller situations, so you gain both self-respect and courage. Let's face it – there are some people in our lives that are way too scary and out of control to be this honest with...yet. But it's not everyone. We learn by practice and there isn't a mountain climber alive that would take on Mt. Everest their first time out. So don't you do that, either! Start with your friends or family or the less scary folks in your life. Practice makes perfect, so practice! Once you've gained a measure of self-confidence, those really scary people will be either easy to approach – or to finally walk away from.

A bit of a twist to back tracking is also effective against Disaster Mind. It's still about pushing yourself towards the truth – but with an added twist. My Disaster Mind loved to convince me that the noises outside my house were someone trying to break in, and not animals. My mind knew it was animals, but my Disaster Mind insisted that people were outside and my life and property were in danger. I would then spin into remarkable levels of fear and anxiety. Yet, I *knew* it was animals. War ensued, Disaster Mind won.

What I finally did was force myself out of bed to grab a flashlight and go outside and walk around the house. Nothing was there (except animals) any of the dozen times I had to do this before my Parasite HATED it so much that my Disaster Mind stopped…at least with this. Once a year it will try again, and all I have to say to myself is, "I'm going to take The Walk", and it shuts up! (Note: I KNEW it was squirrels, which made this a safe experiment to run. Do not, I repeat DO NOT, do something like this if there is any question for your safety!)

If your mind wants to tell that white lie, remind it you have to backtrack and fess up after. If you want to eat that cheesecake when it isn't right for you, tell yourself you'll have to run four miles to work it off. If you're thinking you should hide, make a rule that you'll have to 'out' yourself if you do. In every case, though, hold to your commitment to yourself and fess up when you mess up. If you don't, your parasite will let that slip become a wide chasm of excuses as to why you don't have to fess up.

I meant it when I said that your Parasite will HATE this tool. Remember - your Parasite's primary goals are to be safe and *right*, right? I think you can now see how simply *threatening* to back-track (and admit that you were wrong) could be enough to keep your Parasite from misbehaving in the first place. And that is a blessing, so give this tool a try!

Booty Boppers

From the title of this section, you might not guess that I'm talking about helpers, here. In my Toltec circles we started calling the friends and support people we share growth processes with 'butt kickers'. My beloved friend and butt kicker, Rainbow, suggested we rename these support people 'booty boppers', which is a much cuter term.

A booty bopper or butt kicker is someone who can understand you, so they usually have a similar urge toward growth and self-awareness. They are there to listen to you, to get to know you and to support you as you begin the work of potty training your brain. It's a mutual relationship, so you get to know and support them, too. You both want to potty train your brains. You meet or call each other a couple of times a month and share your progress. You know the language, the concepts and the tools; and you can often see more clearly when your booty bopper has stepped into a mental trap, distraction or misunderstanding than they can. You help each other out. You remind each other to flush.

It can be as simple as a one hour phone call once or twice a month. You each have a half an hour to share what's been going on. You can commiserate, you can support, you can share insights and you can question each other as to whether you've been flushing....or holding on to...your poop.

If you live in the wilds with no one anywhere near and no friends alive, well, there are coaches and support groups everywhere, and many connect by phone - so, no excuse! Reach out, get support and find a Booty Bopper!

Question *EVERYTHING!*

This saying is a relic from the '60's or '70's and it is still true today. Question every single thing! What others say, what I say, and especially what your mind says. Learn to not operate on rote habit, knee-jerk reaction or out of conformity. Run experiments. Check things out. Use all of your senses. Does it *feel* true? Make no assumptions. Stop saying 'I know' – because as soon as you do you have stopped learning, stopped questioning and stopped exploring. I know you think you know – but this kind of thinking is a death trap for growth.

This questioning of everything to find your own truth doesn't have to take forever, but have patience. It's the practice of a lifetime, and you've never done it before. So many beliefs were accepted simply because someone we thought of as an authority figure, godhead or minor deity told us they were true. And *THEY WERE TRUE* – for them. Heck, even that's questionable.

Remember that it's not our thoughts, but our attachment to our thoughts, that causes suffering. We attach and hold onto thoughts when we believe they are true, *without questioning them.* You have got to question your cherished assumptions, the ideas you hold close and everything you've accepted on faith. You may find they are still true for you – or not – but you won't know until you look.

Fire does not always burn! The world is not flat! Nothing is really solid! Man can fly! There is no control! Animals aren't dumb! We don't die from love! Humans aren't the only intelligent life on earth! Question every assumption, belief and idea you have!

Brain on Crack and Stress

Ever see those anti-drug commercials where they show you an egg and say, 'this is your brain', then they crack the egg into a hot frying pan and you watch it sizzling as they say, 'and this is your brain on crack'? Well, our poor brains also fry when subjected to fatigue, stress, illness, grief and more.

Don Miguel's book, *The Four Agreements,* is really worth a read if you haven't, yet. One of the agreements is to always do your best, understanding that your best changes. It changes throughout every hour, day and week of our lives, going up and down, depending on what's happening with our bodies and brains.

Our best in the morning is usually better than our best at night. Our best when we're rested is far better than our best when we're exhausted. Our best when we're not hungry is better than when we are. When we're grieving, we're not usually spot on. Ditto when we're tipsy, depressed, sad, wired, stuffed, scared, overworked, in pain, stressed or angry.

The key here is to understand and accept where your best is in any given moment, and to act and react accordingly. I don't use my chainsaw when I'm tired. It is better not to go to work when you're sick. Having an important or serious conversation when you (or they) are drunk is just plain dumb. Some of us aren't very reasonable when we're scared or threatened. Don't open your mouth if you can't control it (and back-track if you do)!

Give yourself a break when you're not at one hundred percent, and don't expect yourself to be what you're not. You are human, and as humans, our 100% fluctuates. Your Parasite rarely fluctuates and won't give you that break. Your judge will expect you to be sublime no matter what, so it's up to you to bring in loving, wise parental controls and a dose of the truth - and give yourself a break when you're riding the lower percentiles. It's the best you can do under the circumstances and it is *normal* to have ups and downs – no matter what your Parasite says!

Have a Heart

This topic deserves an entire book, yet the short of it is that you have a heart, so use it. And I don't mean with romantic fantasy or bleeding heart liberals or any of the romanticized distortions our culture loves to pander about.

The heart is part of the body, and I've been telling you to listen to your body, yes? Well, listening to your heart takes that tool deeper, but it is essentially the same. Our hearts *know*. Researchers have discovered that our hearts have brain-type cells in them. Our hearts generate their own special energy field. Our hearts can guide us and inform our lives...if we listen and pay attention to the quiet way in which they communicate, or sometimes nudge us.

Humans, though, tend to focus on our mind when it is from our hearts that we get the truth on *what* to do. Our heart knows our dreams, our real goals, our deepest desires and our passions. If we'd listened to our hearts and not our heads, we might have led very different lives, becoming everything we dreamed about.

And, it's not too late, no matter what your Parasite tells you! When your Parasite tries to stop you from listening to your heart and tells you that you'll destroy the life you've spent so much time and energy creating, say: *Oh Bullshit* – it doesn't have to be that way - because it doesn't.

Listening to our hearts often means quieting the mind's chatter. Mind will resist (go figure!), so it can help to imagine your mind as a baby – and stick a pacifier in its mouth, tuck it in a crib, and tell it you'll be back and everything is fine. With regular practice in quieting the mind, it will hush up for a while and give you space. When it wakes up again, simply hug it and stick the pacifier back in and go back to being quiet. In the quiet you achieve, open your heart and ask it – what do I need now? What does my heart want? Then listen and feel.

Our heart often speaks as a feeling, a 'rightness' or a knowing, of what you want or need. Sometimes it communicates as a sensation, sometimes as a one-line thought, and other times simply as an impression. Unlike mind, our heart doesn't chatter on. Often, our heart's desire *is the exact opposite of what we're actually doing*, which is OK – really. It is important to remember that we're working towards *awareness* of our truth, and that being aware does not mean we must take action. It simply means we are now aware and at choice, and that we're no longer blind to our truth.

My heart has been telling me for years to put all my belongings in storage and go on a 'walk-about'. As with Adyashanti's line, my heart hasn't explained itself, it just says go. Right now, though, I'm choosing to teach and coach and not leave my students and clients.

Because I've listened and heard my heart's voice and I know I have choice, I choose to honor its message in other ways. I do small 'walk-abouts'. I take more trips, I go on walks and I explore new places and vistas. For you, let's say your heart tells you that you really want to be an artist but you're a lawyer instead. You can still take a painting class, spend time in museums and art galleries and prepare for retirement when you'll have more time for your heart's desire.

Sometimes, it can be such an awakening when you listen to your heart and remember the passion you always wanted to follow, that you choose to make that change now. That's great, too. I've done it many times with no regrets. There may be dozens of things you need to negotiate in order to follow your heart, but that's OK. You can do it. Don't forget, though, that you've domesticated the people around you and it may come as quite a shock to them when you decide to make changes. They may firmly stand against you. It could also be that the people in your life understand and support you. Or, it could be a mixed bag.

Whatever you choose, remember that you chose it. As you think, you create. My support to you is that you create change in your life in a way that opens your heart, makes you feel good and that is in your integrity. Be firm, but gentle and kind with those around you, just as you'd like them to be with you. If they think you're going crazy, remember that they are talking from their own domestication, blinders and fears. Heck, what you're doing might even sound crazy to you, too – but trust your heart and know that it is simply giving you your true heart's desire. And then run experiments!

In a balanced world, one that hasn't set our minds up to reign supreme, it would be our hearts we followed in choosing *what* we do. Once we know that (what we want), it is then our mind's job to figure out *how* to accomplish it. Mind is really good at figuring out the 'how to', and this is its proper role. If you think about it, given mind's constipation from all of its domestication - why would we let our mind decide our heart's desire and our passions? I mean, really! Listen to your heart's desire and follow that. Mind can then help you with the details.

What Opens You?

This is a fun experience to stalk in yourself. What opens you? What makes your body open, relax and expand? What makes your heart sing? What has your body going '*yes!*', and yes, and yes? Once you see what opens you, you now know what to do – those things that open you.

The flip side is stalking what closes you. What makes you tense up, shut down and anxious? What feels like revulsion in your body? What feels like 'ick'? What has you going, 'no, no, no - please don't make me'? Once you see this, now you know what not to do!

It is so simple, yes? Once you have practiced and gained skill at stalking your body, this exercise gets easy.

Again, we haven't always done what we wanted out of fear of other people's reactions, or our own ideas of 'should'. Humans do tend to 'should ourselves to death' and I wish we'd all just throw that one out. Think about it. Most of our 'shoulds' have come from someone else's ideas of what is right, proper and correct. If we're closing down, that's a clue that it isn't *our* idea – or at least not right for us in the moment. An honest look at how it makes you *feel* to deny or force yourself is often enough to cure this one. I mean, ick is ick and doesn't feel great, so why keep doing things that make you feel crappy?

Having said that, in both cases (opened/closed) you may still do the 'thing', but you did it with awareness so you won't be blaming anyone else for your misery - or your joy. You made a choice, conscious of what you were doing. There are times when we do things we don't want to do, and times we do things despite everyone telling us we shouldn't. No problem! If you think it is easier to go to the family reunion, even though you don't want to – great! Just go and make the best of it. You might be surprised that you enjoy yourself if you're not whining the whole time that somebody else made you go! And if everyone says you're crazy, but it opens you to do something – then do it! I traveled through Asia and had a great, safe time despite everyone telling me I was crazy to go alone.

Learning to watch your body for what opens and closes you is very, very powerful. Remember, our bodies know and sense far more than our minds usually do. It can tell us what our heart wants when our mind gets confused between should, must, have to, don't want to at all, really want to regardless, could be interesting, could be scary, a big deal or boring.

Again, let your heart and what opens you inform *what* you do, and then let your amazing mind figure out *how* to do it. This is the way to assign both heart and mind their proper functions. Of course, I'll be encouraging you to follow your heart and do the things that open you and make all parts of you go *'Yes, Yes, Yes!'*

Gratitude

We spend so much time fretting over what we don't like, don't have and don't want – it's amazing. It is also a waste of time and energy of gigantic proportions, not to mention negative goal setting. Thinking about what you want to change in your life is valuable, but we don't stop at that. Human beings tend to chew, like a terrier, on the bones of our dissention. We feed our dissatisfaction, especially with ourselves, and certainly with everything and everyone around us. By now you've learned that the law of attraction works all of the time, and I am hoping that you have started to shift your thoughts.

To continue that shift, gratitude is one of the most heart centering, expansive techniques around for shifting you right down to your toes. In part, it is around finding the truth. Yes, things might be difficult, but there is *always* more happening in our lives than our difficulty. Everyone has something to be grateful for, and most of us have many things. When is the last time you paused to truly appreciate the partner, child, friend, food, drink, lesson, smile, kiss, car, love, sunlight, rain, the clothes on your back or the fact that you are alive? We all have *something* to be grateful for!

Practicing gratitude helps us shift from the heaviness of life to the lighter, more expansive feelings. A gratitude practice can be as simple as a quiet 'thank you', said or felt with the feeling of real appreciation. The deeper practice that I learned from Tom Kenyon takes an extra minute.

What you do first is focus on your physical heart in your chest. It's almost center, with a tilt to the left. While focusing on your heart, you then bring to mind a situation, person or thing that you're grateful for. It can be a time in the past where someone helped you, a new job, your family, a gift someone gave you or as simple as the meal you are about to eat. It is important at this point to move into *feeling* gratitude – not thinking about gratitude. Bring that feeling of gratitude into your physical heart area and let gratitude fill your heart while you bask in that feeling. This is the first step, filling your heart with gratitude.

Once you can sustain the feeling of gratitude in your heart, you then let it overflow. Let that feeling of gratitude spill out of your heart area and flow into your entire body, which is the second step. I imagine my heart radiating gratitude to every cell in my body, filling me with this wonderful, warm feeling of gratitude.

Once you can spread and sustain the feeling of gratitude throughout your body, the third step is to let it overflow again. Let the gratitude filling you overflow outward around you. Let it fill the kitchen; let it flow through the garage, the office, the café or the woods around you. Imagine gratitude flowing out of you and spreading throughout the area where you are, bathing everything in gratitude.

This practice can take time to do quickly, but it doesn't take long. It is so darned yummy! You might notice that shifts happen around you, other people become aware of something good happening, they react positively and some may approach you if you're in public. If so, that's great. It is not, however, the reason to do this gratitude practice! We don't do this for others, folks! Doing so runs the very real (and large) risk of our becoming self-important and building an arrogant ego.

Do this gratitude practice for you, because you want to shift, because you want to experience the feeling of gratitude and all that it generates *in you*. If others benefit, again, that's great. It should not, however, be the reason you do the practice. The point of this practice is for us to expand and shift our attention and our energy out of our crap and into a place of open, loving appreciation. Doing so can work miracles in your life, and it makes whatever life you're living so much richer. Try it.....you'll love it!

Given my busy life, I looked for ways that I could do this practice regularly because I saw the benefits for my mind and body. I started by 'blessing' and being grateful for the food I eat. I LOVE the food I eat and it is easy for me to be grateful for it – several times a day. I then expanded to appreciating the morning light when I go jogging or the scenery when I'm driving. I appreciate all the seeming synchronicities that happen in my life. I even appreciate green traffic lights. I appreciate the goodness and blessings I receive. I'm practicing gratitude all day, every day, and what I've noticed is that I have more and more to be grateful for, and my heart keeps opening more and more! Filling your life with gratitude means your Parasite has less room manipulate you. What a bonus!

Oh Shit!

Let's face it – shit happens. Accidents and slips happen and suddenly we find ourselves in a hard place. Our minds have been going off on someone, something or ourselves - and hours, even *days,* have gone by. We're really angry, sad, depressed, guilt ridden or confused and can't *believe* we let ourselves do that thing we did. We've been trapped once again by our Parasite and have forgotten to use our tools. Heck, we've forgotten everything we've learned except the thing we've been chewing on or that empty red line.

This will happen to every one of us. Period. You have to remember that you're *in training* here, often learning something you've never done before - like paying attention and being kind to yourself. Accidents, slips and falls happen, so just dust yourself off and begin again – without judgment. Bring in your tools the moment you are aware that you let them slip. Pull out the pacifier and stick it firmly in your Parasite's mouth. Back track. *Suspend the judge and tell it to back off* - you're learning here!

What I've noticed is that our habitual thoughts and behaviors will keep happening, but that hindsight gets shorter. Where we once spent a week beating ourselves or others up, we now catch it in days and then in hours until we find we're catching it before we act. It is a process.

You'll get there. And you'll be a lot happier if you don't beat yourself up along the way.

Ram Dass, a famous Hindu teacher, says that issues still knock on the door – he just doesn't invite them in anymore. He has stopped the sleepovers and long dinners and doesn't even take coffee breaks with his poo. As long as we're alive, issues may still knock – we just don't have to open the door, folks!

So, understand that shit happens – and it's OK. And, when it does, you simply pick yourself and your tools up, give yourself a hug, and begin again. You bring in parental controls to remind you that mistakes are necessary for learning, and then you hit the 'resume' button on your practices. That's all; you just begin again.

Sick and Tired Enough Yet?

For some people, this is exactly what it will take for them to make changes in their lives: they get so sick and tired of all of their crap that they can't take it anymore. Some get tired of all of it, while others will change a few areas of their lives yet be afraid to change others.

It seems to be a truth that some of us will only get ourselves up and at it when we are so sick of what's going on that we feel we have no other choice. It's the end of our rope and we've hit bottom. If that's what it takes, that's what it takes, but - what a hard way to go! Ouch!

Laziness can sometimes slow us down, or there are times when we haven't identified the source of our angst, and so we procrastinate. At other times, things don't seem so bad until we suddenly find ourselves beginning to 'blow', and we do tend to blow when we've reached the 'sick and tired' stage. We've put up, shut up, avoided, denied and pretended for so long that the pressure has built to the boiling over point. Again, exploding isn't very healthy for anyone in our lives – especially us. In most of these cases, we've simply been avoiding, distracting or denying the clues that (I guarantee you) have presented themselves to you through your body and mind, telling you that help or change is needed - now!

It's all OK, folks. At some point you really *will* get so sick and tired of the crap that you'll do something about it. When you reach this point, don't judge yourself (no fault, no blame); just get up, pull out these tools and start. You just start from the bottom or wherever you are. You turn toward what you've buried or avoided and you take a look, ask questions, explore and make different choices. There isn't a magic pill, but these tools will help.

Mountains and Final Thoughts

I have an analogy I use to describe how potty training ourselves works. When you start out on a path of self-awareness and mastery, your poo is like a mountain before you. It's huge, and you can easily see it. You start practicing and learning and digging away at the mountain. It doesn't take that long for the mountain to become a foothill. Then it becomes rolling hills, followed by big boulders, rocks, gravel, sand and dust. Around the gravel stage we begin to think that we're done! Ha!

The thing is, that gravel, sand and dust can be hard to see and will trip you up faster than you can imagine.

Our mountain of poo took our lifetime to get as large as it is. There are habits to change, neural networks to create and reroute and patterns to reprogram. A good rule of thumb that Raven taught me is to give something a year. If that specific poop hasn't arisen in a year, you *might* have finished with it. Then stalk it for another year, and if it hasn't arisen again – you've probably worked it out.

I know, that sounds so *long*! It's a gauge and a tool of when you might have fully shifted a self-limiting thought process or behavior. If you think about it, we're going to live life anyway, so learning and growing is what's important - not the speed we do it in. Having said that, the Toltec path and tools work quickly – as long as you actually use them. A Buddhist Lama in Nepal once told me that I'd attain enlightenment in another lifetime or so. My thought was, "Great – but I want to move faster than that!" These tools will help you move faster.

Another thing to understand is that the Parasite gets 'slippery' and sneaky (the gravel, sand and dust). It learns all the tricks and grows as you do. As you advance or become more spiritual, your Parasite advances, too. Before, when you judged, it was like, OK...I'm judging people. Now that you're getting more aware or more 'spiritual', your parasite will even start to *judge you for judging* because we all know that advanced or spiritual people are supposed to be above all that! You see, it's sneaky. Your Parasite is reading this book with you and learning ways to trick you into old habits to keep itself safe and right. That's OK. As long as you're using these tools, you'll catch it.

The art and mastery of awareness is a life-long, evolving practice. It requires dedication to your truth and freedom. It requires ruthless compassion and parental controls. It also requires the understanding that if our mountain of poo took our lifetime, so far, to get to where it is, well, it will take some time to clear it all out. Contrary to what some might say, it does not have to take forever or many lifetimes, either. You *can* do this here and now, but you have to actually *DO* it to get anywhere.

And here's the beauty of this work – as you clear out more and more gunky poo, *you* get clearer and can hear that quiet voice of your inner wisdom and heart more easily. As you hear your heart and inner wisdom more clearly, you get even more information to take your life to greater heights. The negative self-talk in your head slows down and gets quieter, and the quiet allows your truth and your uniqueness to shine through.

If you make personal integrity, choice, freedom and free will your goals, you can attain them – and so much more. As you think, you create. This book was written to help you understand *how* and *what* you create, so that you can change and reclaim the parts of yourself that have been buried…..and now you know under what!

Understanding how you were domesticated, how we were all domesticated, can open up new levels of awareness and compassion - not only for yourself but for others, too. Once you see the errors, lies and misunderstandings that have created your beliefs, you can change them. You can't change what you can't see – so *look!* We don't have to do this in a vacuum, either. So many people are walking a path of self-discovery these days, go join them. Come out and play! Our changing can open the doors for others to change simply by seeing our example. If one of us can do it, then we all can.

All I am asking you to do is to simply be 'you'. That's right, just you - yet I'm talking about the truth of you without the distortions. When I look at this process in myself, it is clear to me that it has involved a chiseling away of what is 'not me' to reveal what 'is me'. It's like the story of a sculptor creating a masterpiece in stone: he removes everything that isn't the sculpture so that the truth of the piece within the stone is revealed.

I believe it is everyone's birthright to be as bright, amazing and wondrous as they truly are, *and* as they choose to be. What will you choose? Will you choose 'same old, same old' or will you choose to change? Will you follow someone else's 'rules', or follow your own? Will you continue to limit yourself, or will you cut the crap and soar?

Your choice!

Further Reading

Amara, HeatherAsh. *The Toltec Path of Transformation: Embracing the Four Elements of Change.* San Antonio, TX: Hierophant Publishing, 2012.

Bach, Richard. *Illusions: The Adventures of a Reluctant Messiah.* New York: Dell Publishing Co., Inc., 1977.

Castaneda, Carlos. *Journey to Ixtlan: The Lessons of Don Juan.* New York: Simon and Schuster, 1972.

-----. *The Power of Silence: Further Lessons of Don Juan.* New York: Simon and Schuster, 1987.

Chopra, Deepak. *Power, Freedom and Grace: Living from the Source of Lasting Happiness.* San Rafael, CA: Amber-Allen Publishing, 2006.

Katie, Byron. *Loving What Is: Four Questions that can Change Your Life.* New York: Three Rivers Press, 2002.

Ruiz, Miguel. *The Four Agreements: A Practical Guide to Personal Freedom.* San Rafael, CA: Amber-Allen Publishing, 1997.

Ruiz, Jr., Miguel. *The Five Levels of Attachment: Toltec Wisdom for the Modern World.* San Antonio, TX: Hierophant Publishing, 2013.

Vigil, Bernadette. *Mastery of Awareness: Living the Agreements.* Rochester, VT: Bear & Co., 2001.

Diana D. Adkins

Toltec teacher, coach and minister, Diana's passions have taken her around the world - from barns to boardrooms, mountains to monasteries and from seeking to surely finding.

Deeply committed to understanding the nature of 'life, the universe and everything else', Diana brings her training from Buddhism, Christianity, Sufism, Native American Church, Shamanism, Wicca, Judaism, Hinduism, Science and Life to her work. She is a Life and Spiritual Integrity Coach, Reiki Master and is certified in the Law of

Attraction, Rays, the Dervish Healing Order and Shamanic Healing.

A 'recovering accountant', Diana worked as CEO/CFO for non-profits in Idaho, Washington, California, New Mexico and Indonesia. She continues to serve on the Board of Directors for two organizations that are close to her heart: the Lama Foundation and Toci – Toltec Center of Creative Intent.

Visit her web site at www.makeitsacred.com and on Twitter (pottytrainbrain) and her Facebook page for Potty Train Your Brain.

25525460R00086

Made in the USA
Middletown, DE
01 November 2015